FULL STEAM AHEAD

For the Railways of Central & Eastern England 2010-2011

GW00694096

EDITOR
John Robinson

First Edition

RAILWAY LOCATOR MAP

The numbers shown on this map relate to the page numbers for each railway.
Pages 5-6 contain an alphabetical listing of the railways featured in this guide.
Please note that the markers on this map show the approximate location only.

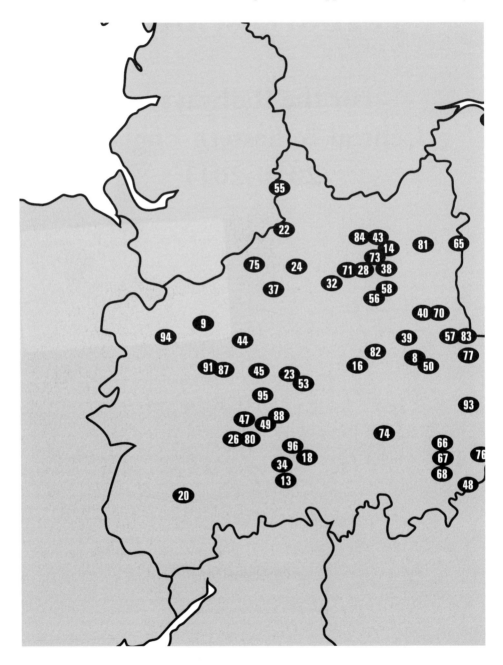

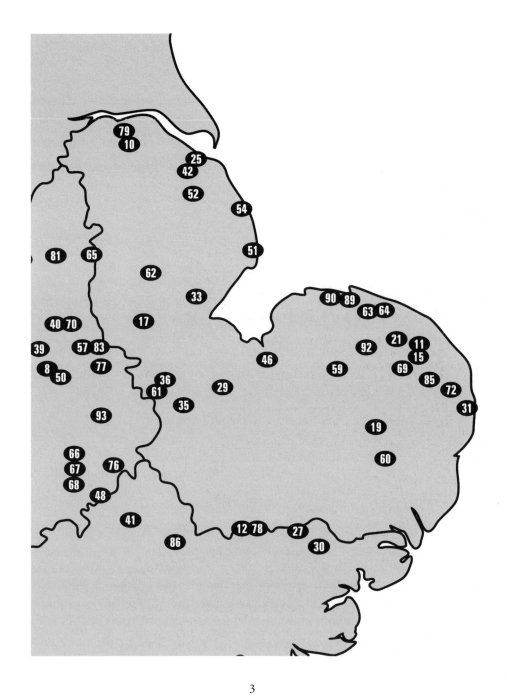

ACKNOWLEDGEMENTS

We were greatly impressed by the friendly and cooperative manner of the staff and helpers of the railways and societies which we selected to appear in this book, and wish to thank them all for the help they have given. In addition we wish to thank Bob Budd (cover design) and Michael Robinson (page layouts) for their help.

We are particularly indebted to Peter Bryant for his invaluable assistance. Peter's web site: www.miniaturerailwayworld.co.uk provides a great deal of information about Miniature Railways in the UK.

Although we believe that the information contained in this guide is accurate at the time of going to press, we, and the Railways and Societies itemised, are unable to accept liability for any loss, damage, distress or injury suffered as a result of any inaccuracies. Furthermore, we and the Societies are unable to guarantee operating and opening times which may always be subject to cancellation without notice.

John Robinson

John Robinson

EDITOR

COVER PHOTOGRAPHS

The railways featured on the front cover are the Midland Railway – Butterley, the Cleethorpes Coast Light Railway and the Wells & Walsingham Light Railway. We are indebted to the Midland Railway for supplying their photo and giving us permission for its use.

British Library Cataloguing in Publication Data
A catalogue record for this book is available from the British Library

ISBN-13: 978-1-86223-195-5

Copyright © 2010, MARKSMAN PUBLICATIONS. (01472 696226)
72 St. Peter's Avenue, Cleethorpes, N.E. Lincolnshire, DN35 8HU, England

All rights are reserved. No part of this publication may be reproduced, stored in a retrieval system or transmitted, in any form or by any means, electronic, mechanical, photocopying, recording, or otherwise, without the prior written permission of Marksman Publications.

The Publishers and respective Railways are unable to accept liability for any loss, damage or injury caused by error or inaccuracy in the information published in this guide.

Printed in the UK by The Cromwell Press Group

FOREWORD

The aim of this series of guides is to showcase the great range of UK railways, large and small. In deciding areas covered by this guide we have tried to stick to county boundaries wherever possible but, in a few cases, railways located close to the borders between counties may appear in both this and other guides in the series!

CONTENTS

ABBEY PUMPING STATION

Address: Abbey Pumping Station Museum, Corporation Road, Leicester, LE4 5PX	**N° of Steam Locos:** 1
	N° of Other Locos: 4
	N° of Members: Approximately 80
Telephone N°: (0116) 299-5111	**Annual Membership Fee:** £8.00 Adult,
Year Formed: 1980s	£10.00 Family
Location of Line: Leicester	**Approx N° of Visitors P.A.:** 60,000
Length of Line: 300 yards	**Gauge:** 2 feet

GENERAL INFORMATION

Nearest Mainline Station: Leicester London Road (3 miles)
Nearest Bus Station: Leicester (1½ miles)
Car Parking: Free parking available on site (Free parking at the Space Centre on Special Event days)
Coach Parking: Use the Space Centre car park
Souvenir Shop(s): Yes
Food & Drinks: Available on special event days only

SPECIAL INFORMATION

The Museum is situated in the Abbey Pumping Station which, from 1891 to 1964 pumped Leicester's sewage to nearby treatment works. The Museum now collects and displays the industrial, technological and scientific heritage of Leicester and contains rare working examples of Woolf compound rotative beam engines which are in steam on selected days.

OPERATING INFORMATION

Opening Times: The Pumping Station is open daily from February to October, 11.00am to 4.30pm. Trains run on the first Saturday of each month from April and during some special events, 1.00pm to 5.00pm.
Steam Working: Selected special event days only. Please contact the Museum for further details.
Prices: Adults £3.50 (Special event days only)
Concessions £2.50 (Special events only)
Family £8.00 (Special event days only)

Detailed Directions by Car:
From All Parts: The Museum is situated next to the National Space Centre, about 1 mile North of Leicester city centre near Beaumont Leys and Belgrave. Brown tourist signs with a distinctive rocket logo provide directions to the NSC from the arterial routes around Leicester and the Museum is nearby.

AMERTON RAILWAY

Address: Amerton Farm, Stow-by-Chartley, Staffordshire ST18 0LA	**N° of Steam Locos**: 2
Telephone N°: (01785) 850965	**N° of Other Locos**: 7
Year Formed: 1991	**N° of Members**: 45
Location: Amerton Farm	**Approx N° of Visitors P.A.**: 30,000
Length of Line: Approximately 1 mile	**Gauge**: 2 feet
	Web site: www.amertonrailway.co.uk

GENERAL INFORMATION

Nearest Mainline Station: Stafford (8 miles)
Nearest Bus Station: Stafford (8 miles)
Car Parking: Free parking available on site
Coach Parking: Available by arrangement
Souvenir Shop(s): Yes
Food & Drinks: Yes

SPECIAL INFORMATION

The Railway is run by volunteers and the circuit was completed in 2002. The Summer Steam Gala in 2010 will be held on 19th & 20th June.

OPERATING INFORMATION

Opening Times: Weekends from the end of March to the end of October and on Tuesdays, Wednesdays and Thursdays during the School Holidays. Also open for Santa Specials in December. Open from midday to 5.00pm at weekends but only until 4.00pm during midweek dates.
Steam Working: Sundays and Bank Holidays only.
Prices: Adult £2.10
Child £1.40
Concession £1.60

Detailed Directions by Car:
Amerton is located on the A518, 1 mile from the junction with the A51 – Amerton Farm is signposted at the junction. The Railway is located approximately 8 miles from Junction 14 of the M6.

Appleby Frodingham R.P.S.

Address: Appleby Frodingham Railway Preservation Society, P.O. Box 44, Brigg, North Lincolnshire DN20 8XG
Telephone Nº: (01652) 656661
Year Formed: 1990
Location of Line: Corus Steelworks, Scunthorpe

Length of Line: 15 miles used on tours from almost 100 miles of track
Nº of Steam Locos: 2
Nº of Other Locos: 3
Nº of Members: 60
Gauge: Standard
Web site: www.afrps.co.uk

GENERAL INFORMATION

Nearest Mainline Station: Scunthorpe (1 mile)
Nearest Bus Station: Scunthorpe (½ mile)
Car Parking: Large free car park at the site
Coach Parking: At the site
Souvenir Shop(s): Yes – at the Loco Shed
Food & Drinks: Drinks/snacks served on train trips

SPECIAL INFORMATION

The Society operates 8 and 15 mile Rail and Brake Van tours of the Corus steelworks site (which covers almost 12 square miles) using its extensive internal railway system.

OPERATING INFORMATION

Opening Times: Selected weekends throughout the year which must be pre-booked via (01652) 657053 or e-mail – bookings@afrps.co.uk
Private Hire of a train is now available for parties and anniversaries with use of the Lounge coach.
Steam Working: Most active days. Ask for further details when booking.
Prices: Free – but the society relies on donations which are collected at the end of each tour.
Please note that children cannot be carried on Brake van tours due to the open verandahs.

Detailed Directions by Car:
Exit the M180 at Junction 4 and take the A18 into Scunthorpe. Turn right at the roundabout by Morrisons supermarket and follow the road along for approximately ½ mile. Turn right into Entrance E. Car parking is available on the left and the path to the station is on the right.

ASHMANHAUGH LIGHT RAILWAY

Address: East View Farm, Stone Lane, Ashmanhaugh, Norwich   NR12 8YW
Telephone N°: (01603) 404263
Year Formed: 2002
Location of Line: Near Wroxham Barns
Length of Line: 900 yards

N° of Steam Locos: 2
N° of Other Locos: 5
N° of Members: –
Approx N° of Visitors P.A.: 2,500
Gauge: 7¼ inches
Web site:
www.ashmanhaughlightrailway.co.uk

GENERAL INFORMATION

Nearest Mainline Station: Wroxham & Hoveton (1½ miles)
Nearest Bus Station: Norwich (10 miles)
Car Parking: Available on site
Coach Parking: None
Souvenir Shop(s): None
Food & Drinks: Teas and drinks only

SPECIAL INFORMATION

Close to the Bure Valley Line, this is a railway operated by enthusiasts set in the beautiful North Norfolk countryside.

OPERATING INFORMATION

Opening Times: 2010 dates: The first Sunday in the month from 2nd May to 3rd October, weather permitting. Trains run from 2.00pm to 5.00pm.
Steam Working: Most operating days.
Prices: Adults £1.00 (Day Rover ticket £3.00)
Children £1.00 (Day Rover ticket £3.00)
Family Day Rover £10.00 (Unlimited rides)

Detailed Directions by Car:
From All Parts: Ashmanhaugh is situated just off the A1151 Wroxham to Stalham road. The railway is close to the Wroxham Barns Centre and is signposted from the road on open days.

AUDLEY END STEAM RAILWAY

Address: Audley End, Saffron Walden, Essex	**Length of Line**: 1½ miles
Telephone Nº: (01799) 541354	**Nº of Steam Locos**: 6
Year Formed: 1964	**Nº of Other Locos**: 3
Location of Line: Opposite Audley End House, Saffron Walden	**Nº of Members**: None
	Approx Nº of Visitors P.A.: 42,000
	Gauge: 10¼ inches
	Web site: www.audley-end-railway.co.uk

GENERAL INFORMATION

Nearest Mainline Station: Audley End (1 mile)
Nearest Bus Station: Saffron Walden (1 mile)
Car Parking: Available on site
Coach Parking: Available on site
Souvenir Shop(s): Yes
Food & Drinks: Snacks available

SPECIAL INFORMATION

Audley End Steam Railway is Lord Braybrooke's private miniature railway situated just next to Audley End House, an English Heritage site. Private parties can be catered for outside of normal running hours.

OPERATING INFORMATION

Opening Times: 2010 dates: Weekends from 27th March to 31st October and also daily during School Holidays. Also Santa Specials in December. Trains run from 2.00pm (11.00am on Bank Holidays).
Steam Working: Weekends and Bank Holidays.
Prices: Adult Return £3.50
             Child Return £2.50
             Santa Specials £5.00
Note: Multi-ride tickets are also available.

Detailed Directions by Car:
Exit the M11 at Junction 10 if southbound or Junction 9 if northbound and follow the signs for Audley End House. The railway is situated just across the road from Audley End House.

Avonvale Model Engineering Society

Address: Hillers, Dunnington, Warwickshire B49 5PD	**N° of Steam Locos**: 16
Phone N°: (01242) 675219 (Secretary)	**N° of Other Locos**: 12
Year Formed: 2001	**N° of Members**: Approximately 40
Location of Line: Hillers, Dunnington	**Approx N° of Visitors P.A.**: 3,000
Length of Line: A third of a mile	**Gauge**: 5 inches and 7¼ inches

GENERAL INFORMATION

Nearest Mainline Station: Evesham (11 miles)
Nearest Bus Station: Stratford-upon-Avon (13 miles)
Car Parking: Free parking available on site
Coach Parking: None
Souvenir Shop(s): None
Food & Drinks: Available

SPECIAL INFORMATION

The Engines are all privately owned and run as required. The railway is located at Hillers where other attractions include a Café, a Farm Shop and a Display Garden.

OPERATING INFORMATION

Opening Times: All Bank Holiday Mondays and also on two other weekends per month from April to October. Please contact the railway for details about operating dates and times.
Steam Working: Where possible at least two steam locos run on each operating day.
Prices: 70p per ride per person.

Detailed Directions by Car:
From the North: Take the A435 or A46 to Alcester then follow the B4088 to Dunnington. Once in Dunnington, turn right at the crossroad and Hillers is on the right hand side with the railway visible from the road; From the South: Take the Evesham bypass then follow the B4088 to Dunnington.

BARROW HILL ROUNDHOUSE RAILWAY CENTRE

Address: Barrow Hill Roundhouse, Campbell Drive, Barrow Hill, Staveley, Chesterfield   S43 2PR
Telephone Nº: (01246) 472450
Year Formed: 1998
Location: Staveley, near Chesterfield
Length of Line: ¾ mile

Nº of Steam Locos: 9
Nº of Other Locos: Over 40
Nº of Members: Approximately 400
Annual Membership Fee: £16.00 (Adult)
Approx Nº of Visitors P.A.: 30,000
Gauge: Standard
Web site: www.barrowhill.org

GENERAL INFORMATION

Nearest Mainline Station:
Chesterfield (3½ miles)
Nearest Bus Station:
Chesterfield (3 miles)
Car Parking: Space available for 300 cars
Coach Parking: Available
Souvenir Shop(s): Yes
Food & Drinks: Yes – buffet

SPECIAL INFORMATION

Britain's last remaining operational railway roundhouse provides storage and repair facilities for standard gauge steam, diesel and electric locomotives.

OPERATING INFORMATION

Opening Times: Open at weekends throughout the year from 10.00am to 4.00pm.
Steam Working: Special open days only. 2010 dates – Rail Ale Festival on 21st & 22nd May; Santa Steam Trains on 12th and 19th December.
Please phone for further details or check the railway's web site.
Prices: Please phone for prices.

Detailed Directions by Car:
Exit the M1 at Junction 30 and take the A619 to Staveley (about 3½ miles). Pass through Staveley, turn right at Troughbrook onto 'Works Road'. Continue along for ¾ mile, pass under the railway bridge and take the turn immediately on the right. Turn left onto Campbell Drive and the Roundhouse is on the left. The railway is signposted with Brown Tourist signs.

Barton House Railway

<table>
<tr><td>

Address: Hartwell Road, The Avenue, Wroxham NR12 8TL
Telephone Nº: (01603) 782470 or (01603) 783569
Year Formed: 1963
Location of Line: Wroxham, Norfolk
Length of Line: 167 yards

</td><td>

Nº of Steam Locos: 4
Nº of Other Locos: 4
Nº of Members: –
Approx Nº of Visitors P.A.: 1,250
Gauge: 3½ inches and 7¼ inches
Web site: www.bartonhouserailway.org.uk

</td></tr>
</table>

GENERAL INFO

Nearest Mainline Station:
Hoveton and Wroxham (1 mile)
Nearest Bus Station:
Wroxham (1 mile)
Car Parking: Limited parking available on site
Coach Parking: None
Souvenir Shop(s): Yes
Food & Drinks: Available

SPECIAL INFO

The original Honing East signalbox was rebuilt at Wroxham to form the basis for the Barton House Railway which is run entirely by volunteers.

OPERATING INFO

Opening Times: The 3rd Sunday each month from April until October and also on Easter Monday. Trains run from 2.30pm to 5.30pm.
Steam Working:
Most operating days.
Prices: Adults £2.00 (by road)
    Children £1.00 (by road)
or   Adults £3.00 (by launch)
    Child £1.50 (by launch)
Note: On open days, access to the railway is also available via an electric launch service running from Wroxham Bridge. Prices of this service are shown above.

Detailed Directions by Car:
From the South and West: Take the A1151 from Norwich to Wroxham then follow the road over the railway bridge. Take the 3rd turning on the right into 'The Avenue', 2nd left into Staitheway Road then right into Hartwell Road. The railway is at the end of the road; From the North: Take the A149 to the A1151 to Wroxham, turn left into 'The Avenue', then as above.

THE BATTLEFIELD LINE

Address: The Battlefield Line, Shackerstone Station, Shackerstone, Warwickshire CV13 6NW	**N° of Steam Locos:** 5
Telephone N°: (01827) 880754	**N° of Other Locos:** 23
Year Formed: 1968	**N° of Members:** 500 approximately
Location of Line: North West of Market Bosworth	**Annual Membership Fee:** £15.00 Adult; £25.00 Family
Length of Line: 5 miles	**Approx N° of Visitors P.A.:** 50,000
	Gauge: Standard
	Web site: www.battlefield-line-railway.co.uk

GENERAL INFORMATION

Nearest Mainline Station: Nuneaton (9 miles)
Nearest Bus Station: Nuneaton & Hinckley (9 miles)
Car Parking: Ample free parking available
Coach Parking: Can cater for coach parties
Souvenir Shop(s): Yes
Food & Drinks: Yes – Station Buffet

SPECIAL INFORMATION

Travel from the Grade II listed Shackerstone Station through the beautiful Leicestershire countryside with views of the adjoining Ashby Canal. Arrive at the award-winning Shenton Station and explore Bosworth Battlefield (1485) before making the return journey.

OPERATING INFORMATION

Operating Info: 2010 dates: Weekends and Bank Holidays from 20th March to 31st October and Santa Specials on weekends from 4th December to Christmas Eve. Also open on Wednesday afternoons in July and August. Please check the web site for further details.
Opening Times: 10.55am to 5.10pm
Steam Working: From 11.30am to 4.00pm during high season and Sundays.
Prices: Adult Return £8.00
Child Return £5.00 (ages 5-15 years)
O.A.P. Return £6.50
Family Ticket £24.00
(2 adults and 2 children)

Detailed Directions by Car:
Follow the brown tourist signs from the A444 or A447 heading towards the market town of Market Bosworth. Continue towards the villages of Congerstone & Shackerstone and finally to Shackerstone Station. Access is only available via the Old Trackbed.

BELTON LIGHT RAILWAY

Address: Belton House, Grantham,
NG32 2LS
Telephone N°: (01476) 566116
Year Formed: Not known
Location of Line: Belton House
Length of Line: 500 yards

N° of Steam Locos: None
N° of Other Locos: 1
Approx N° of Visitors P.A.: 248,000 (to
Belton House); 32,000 train journeys
Gauge: 7¼ inches
Web site:
www.nationaltrust.org.uk/beltonhouse

GENERAL INFORMATION

Nearest Mainline Station: Grantham (3 miles)
Nearest Bus Station: Grantham (3 miles)
Car Parking: Available on site
Coach Parking: Available
Souvenir Shop(s): National Trust Shop on site
Food & Drinks: Available

SPECIAL INFORMATION

The railway is located within the grounds of the
historic stately home, Belton House, which is a
National Trust location.

OPERATING INFORMATION

Opening Times: Daily from 3rd March to 31st
October but closed on Mondays and Tuesdays in
March, April, May, June, September and October).
Also open on selected dates in November and
December. Trains run from 10.30am to 5.30pm.
Steam Working: None at present.
Prices: £1.00 per ride
Note: Admission to the house and grounds is an
additional charge.

Detailed Directions by Car:
From All Parts: Belton House is located 3 miles to the North East of Grantham by the side of the A607 Grantham
to Lincoln road and is clearly signposted from the A1 near Grantham.

BIRMINGHAM SOCIETY OF MODEL ENGINEERS

Address: Illshaw Heath Road,
Hockley Heath, Solihull   B94 6DN
Telephone Nº: (01564) 703444
Year Formed: 1936
Location of Line: Solihull
Length of Line: 350 yards (raised track)
and 370 yards (ground-level track)

Nº of Steam Locos: 2
Nº of Other Locos: 3
Nº of Members: Approximately 140
Annual Membership Fee: –
Approx Nº of Visitors P.A.: 1,000+
Gauge: 3½ inches, 5 inches & 7¼ inches
Web site: www.birminghamsme.com

GENERAL INFORMATION

Nearest Mainline Station: Earlswood (3½ miles)
Nearest Bus Station: Solihull (4 miles)
Car Parking: Available on site
Coach Parking: Available
Souvenir Shop(s): None
Food & Drinks: Available

SPECIAL INFORMATION

Founded in 1936, the Birmingham Society of Model
Engineers has grown over the past seventy years to
become a club with one of the largest memberships
in the United Kingdom. The Ilshaw Heath site has

excellent facilities with footbridges, Stations, paved
platforms, signal boxes, steaming bays and an engine
shed in addition to a brick built, double arched
tunnel which spans the two tracks.

OPERATING INFORMATION

Opening Times: The site is open to the public just a
few times each year when train rides are offered.
2010 dates: 14th June. Please check the Society's
web site for further details.
Steam Working: Every operating day.
Prices: Adults 50p per ride
    Children 50p per ride

Detailed Directions by Car:
From All Parts: Exit the M42 at Junction 4 and take the A3400 towards Stratford-upon-Avon. Turn right at the
first roundabout towards Illshaw Heath Village then right again at the crossroads and the railway is located on the
left after approximately 150 yards.

BRESSINGHAM STEAM EXPERIENCE

Address: Bressingham Steam Museum, Bressingham, Diss, Norfolk   IP22 2AB
Telephone Nº: (01379) 686900
Year Formed: Mid 1950's
Location of Line: Bressingham, Near Diss
Length of Line: 5 miles in total (3 lines)

Nº of Steam Locos: Many Steam locos
Nº of Members: 70 volunteers
Annual Membership Fee: –
Approx Nº of Visitors P.A.: 80,000+
Gauge: Standard, 2 foot, 10¼ inches and 15 inches
Web site: www.bressingham.co.uk

GENERAL INFORMATION

Nearest Mainline Station: Diss (2½ miles)
Nearest Bus Station: Bressingham (1¼ miles)
Car Parking: Free parking for 400 cars available
Coach Parking: Free parking for 30 coaches
Souvenir Shop(s): Yes
Food & Drinks: Yes

SPECIAL INFORMATION

In addition to Steam locomotives, Bressingham has a large selection of steam traction engines, fixed steam engines and also the National Dad's Army Museum, two extensive gardens and a water garden centre.

OPERATING INFORMATION

Opening Times: 2010 dates: Daily from 27th March to 31st October. Open from 10.30am to 5.00pm and until 5.30pm in June, July and August.
Steam Working: Almost every operating day except for most Mondays and Tuesdays in March, April, May, June, July, September and October. Please phone the Museum for further details.
Prices: Adult £9.50 (non-Steam) £12.00 (Steam)
Child £6.50 (non-Steam) £8.00 (Steam)
Family £27 (non-Steam) £35.00 (Steam)
Seniors £9.00 (non-Steam) £10.50 (Steam)

Detailed Directions by Car:
From All Parts: Take the A11 to Thetford and then follow the A1066 towards Diss for Bressingham. The Museum is signposted by the brown tourist signs.

BROOMY HILL RAILWAY

Address: Broomy Hill, Hereford	**Nº of Steam Locos**: 4+
Telephone Nº: (01989) 762119	**Nº of Other Locos**: 1+
Year Formed: 1962	**Nº of Members**: Approximately 80
Location of Line: Adjacent to the	**Approx Nº of Visitors P.A.**: Not known
Waterworks Museum, Hereford	**Gauge**: 7¼ inches, 5 inches, 3½ inches
Length of Line: 1 kilometre	**Web site**: www.hsme.co.uk

GENERAL INFORMATION

Nearest Mainline Station: Hereford (1½ miles)
Nearest Bus Station: Hereford (1½ miles)
Car Parking: Free parking available on site
Coach Parking: Available by prior arrangement
Souvenir Shop(s): Yes
Food & Drinks: Available

SPECIAL INFORMATION

The Broomy Hill Railway is operated by the
Hereford Society of Model Engineers and has two
separate tracks which run along the bank of the
River Wye. Members run their own locomotives so
the number and variety in operation may vary from
day to day. Entry to the site is free of charge and
picnic areas are available.

OPERATING INFORMATION

Opening Times: The second and last Sundays of
the month from Easter until September/October.
Trains run from 12.00pm to 4.30pm.
Steam Working: All operating days.
Prices: Adults £1.50 per ride
         Children £1.50 per ride
Note: Four rides can be bought for £5.00

Detailed Directions by Car:
From the centre of Hereford, take the A49 Ross-on-Wye Road, turning right into Barton Road. After approximately
400 metres, turn left into Broomy Hill Road, proceed for around 600 metres before turning left following signs
for the Waterworks Museum. The railway is on the right just after the museum which is signposted with Brown
Tourist Information Signs.

BURE VALLEY RAILWAY

Address: Aylsham Station, Norwich Road, Aylsham, Norfolk NR11 6BW
Telephone Nº: (01263) 733858
Year Formed: 1989
Location of Line: Between Aylsham and Wroxham
Length of Line: 9 miles

Nº of Steam Locos: 5
Nº of Other Locos: 3
Approx Nº of Visitors P.A.: 120,000
Gauge: 15 inches
Web Site: www.bvrw.co.uk
e-mail: info@bvrw.co.uk

GENERAL INFO

Nearest Mainline Station:
Wroxham (adjacent)
Nearest Bus Station:
Aylsham (bus passes station)
Car Parking: Free parking at Aylsham and Wroxham Stations
Coach Parking: As above
Souvenir Shop(s): Yes at both Stations
Food & Drinks: Yes (a Café at Aylsham also opens daily)

SPECIAL INFO

Boat trains connect at Wroxham with a 1½ hour cruise on the Norfolk Broads. Steam Locomotive driving courses are available throughout the year except in July and August. Some carriages are able to carry wheelchairs.

OPERATING INFO

Opening Times: Aylsham Station is open daily. Trains run on various dates in 2010 from 13th February to the end of October. Open during weekends in March and daily from 27th March to 31st October plus some other dates. Trains run from 9.25am to 6.15pm during high season. Open for Santa Specials on dates in December. Please contact the railway for further details.
Steam Working:
Most trains are steam hauled
Prices: Adult Return £11.50
           (Single £7.50)
         Child Return £6.50
           (Single £5.00)
         Family Return £30.00
           (2 adult + 2 child)
Party discounts are available for groups of 20 or more if booked in advance.

Detailed Directions by Car:
From Norwich: Aylsham Station is situated midway between Norwich and Cromer on the A140 – follow the signs for Aylsham Town Centre. Wroxham Station is adjacent to the Wroxham British Rail Station – take the A1151 from Norwich; From King's Lynn: Take the A148 and B1354 to reach Aylsham Station.
Satellite Navigation: Use NR11 6BW for Aylsham Station and NR12 8UU for Wroxham Station.

BUXTON MINIATURE RAILWAY

Address: Pavilion Gardens,
St. John's Road, Buxton   SK17 6XN
Telephone Nº: (01298) 23114
Year Formed: 1972
Location of Line: Buxton, Derbyshire
Length of Line: 320 yards

Nº of Steam Locos: None
Nº of Other Locos: 1
Nº of Members: None
Approx Nº of Visitors P.A.: Not known
Gauge: 12¼ inches
Web site: www.paviliongardens.co.uk

GENERAL INFORMATION

Nearest Mainline Station: Buxton (350 yards)
Nearest Bus Station: Buxton
Car Parking: Available on site – Pay & Display
Coach Parking: Available
Souvenir Shop(s): Yes
Food & Drinks: Available

SPECIAL INFORMATION

The railway is located in the Buxton Pavilion
Gardens, an historic venue of 23 acres situated in the
heart of Buxton which was first opened in 1871.

OPERATING INFORMATION

Opening Times: Weekends throughout the year,
weather permitting and daily during the school
holidays. Open from 10.00am to 4.30pm.
Steam Working: None at present.
Prices: Adults £1.00
            Children £1.00 (Under-3s ride for free)

Detailed Directions by Car:
From All Parts: The railway is located in Pavilion Gardens in Buxton which is at the side of the A53 (St. John's
Road) and just opposite the junction with the A5004 (Manchester Road).

CHASEWATER RAILWAY

Address: Chasewater Country Park, Pool Road, Near Brownhills, Staffs, WS8 7NL
Telephone Nº: (01543) 452623
Year Re-formed: 1985
Location of Line: Chasewater Country Park, Brownhills, near Walsall
Length of Line: 2 miles

Nº of Steam Locos: 10
Nº of Other Locos: 12
Nº of Members: 800
Annual Membership Fee: Adult £15.00; Family £20.00; Concessions £10.00
Approx Nº of Visitors P.A.: 46,000
Gauge: Standard
Web site: www.chaserail.com

GENERAL INFORMATION

Nearest Mainline Station: Walsall or Birmingham (both approximately 8 miles)
Nearest Bus Station: Walsall or Birmingham
Car Parking: Free parking in Chasewater Park
Coach Parking: Free parking in Chasewater Park
Souvenir Shop(s): Yes
Food & Drinks: Yes

SPECIAL INFORMATION

Chasewater Railway is based on the Cannock Chase & Wolverhampton Railway opened in 1856. The railway passed into the hands of the National Coal Board which then ceased using the line in 1965. Trains operate between Brownhills West and Chasetown.

OPERATING INFORMATION

Opening Times: 2010 dates: Sundays and Bank Holiday Mondays throughout the year plus most Saturdays from 22nd May to 11th September and Tuesdays and Thursdays from 27th July to 2nd September. Also Santa Specials in December. A regular service runs from 11.00am on operating days.

Steam Working: Please check the web site or phone for further details.

Prices: Adult Return £3.45
Child Return £2.45
Family Return £8.45

All tickets offer unlimited rides on the day of issue.

Detailed Directions by Car:
Chasewater Country Park is situated in Brownhills off the A5 southbound near the junction of the A5 with the A452 Chester Road. Follow the Brown tourist signs on the A5 for the Country Park.

CHURNET VALLEY RAILWAY

Address: The Railway Station,
Cheddleton, Leek, Staffs. ST13 7EE
Telephone Nº: (01538) 360522
Year Formed: 1978
Location of Line: Cheddleton to Froghall
Length of Line: 5½ miles

Nº of Steam Locos: 2
Nº of Other Locos: 3
Nº of Members: –
Annual Membership Fee: £14.00
Approx Nº of Visitors P.A.: 70,000
Gauge: Standard
Web site: www.churnetvalleyrailway.co.uk

GENERAL INFORMATION

Nearest Mainline Station: Stoke-on-Trent
(12 miles)
Nearest Bus Station: Leek (5 miles)
Car Parking: Parking available on site
Coach Parking: Restricted space – please book in
advance
Souvenir Shop(s): Yes
Food & Drinks: Yes

SPECIAL INFORMATION

Cheddleton Station is a Grade II listed building,
Consall is a sleepy halt with Victorian charm, whereas
Kingsley & Froghall has been rebuilt in NSR style and
includes disabled facilities and a tearoom.

OPERATING INFORMATION

Opening Times: 2010 dates: Weekends and Bank
Holidays from 2nd April to 10th October. Also open
on Wednesdays in July, August and December and
on weekends in December. Trains run from 10.30am
on most operating days or from 10.00am on Bank
Holidays and Special Event days.
Steam Working: Sundays from March to October,
Saturdays from May to September, Wednesdays in
July and August and all Bank Holiday Mondays. Also
various other special events throughout the year.
Prices: Please telephone (01538) 360522 for details
or check the railway's web site.

Detailed Directions by Car:
From All Parts: Take the M6 to Stoke-on-Trent and follow trunk roads to Leek. Cheddleton Station is just off the
A520 Leek to Stone road. Kingsley & Froghall Station is just off the A52 Ashbourne Road.

CLEETHORPES COAST LIGHT RAILWAY

Address: King's Road, Cleethorpes, North East Lincolnshire   DN35 0AG
Telephone Nº: (01472) 604657
Year Formed: 1948
Location of Line: Lakeside Park & Marine embankment along Cleethorpes seafront
Length of Line: Almost 2 miles

Nº of Steam Locos: 9
Nº of Other Locos: 4
Nº of Members: 200
Annual Membership Fee: Adult £11.00
Approx Nº of Visitors P.A.: 120,000
Gauge: 15 inches
Web: www.cleethorpescoastlightrailway.co.uk

GENERAL INFORMATION

Nearest Mainline Station: Cleethorpes (1 mile)
Nearest Bus Stop: Meridian Point (opposite)
Car Parking: Boating Lake car park – 500 spaces (fee charged)
Coach Parking: As above
Souvenir Shop(s): Yes
Food & Drinks: Brief Encounters Tearoom on Lakeside Station

SPECIAL INFORMATION

A line extension to Humberston opened in 2008.

OPERATING INFORMATION

Opening Times: 2010 dates: Open daily from 30th April to 12th September. Also open on weekends, Bank holidays and school holidays at all other times, 11.00am to 4.20pm in Winter, 6.00pm in Summer.
Steam Working: Weekends throughout the year and daily from March to October.
Prices: Adult Return £3.90
            Child Return £3.50
            Family Return £12.00 (2 Adult + 2 Child)
Note: Lower prices apply for shorter journeys.

Detailed Directions by Car:
Take the M180 to the A180 and continue to its' end. Follow signs for Cleethorpes. The Railway is situated along Cleethorpes seafront 1 mile south of the Pier. Look for the brown Railway Engine tourist signs and the main station is adjacent to the Leisure Centre.

COALYARD MINIATURE RAILWAY

Address: c/o Severn Valley Railway, Comberton Road, Kidderminster, DY10 1QX
Telephone Nº: (0121) 552-5148
Year Formed: 1988
Location of Line: Kidderminster Town Station at the Severn Valley Railway

Length of Line: 500 yards
Nº of Steam Locos: 1 (+ visiting locos)
Nº of Other Locos: 2 (+ visiting locos)
Nº of Members: 12
Approx Nº of Visitors P.A.: 16,000
Gauge: 7¼ inches

GENERAL INFORMATION

Nearest Mainline Station: Kidderminster (adjacent)
Nearest Bus Station: Kidderminster (¼ mile)
Car Parking: Pay & Display car park is adjacent
Coach Parking: Available
Souvenir Shop(s): Severn Valley Railway Shop is adjacent
Food & Drinks: Available from the adjacent Kidderminster Museum and Severn Valley Railway Restaurant.

SPECIAL INFORMATION

The Coalyard Miniature Railway is based at the Severn Valley Railway's Kidderminster Town Station and raises funds for the Station and other projects on the Severn Valley Railway.

OPERATING INFORMATION

Opening Times: Most Saturdays, Sundays and Bank Holidays throughout the year. Please contact the railway for further information.
Steam Working: On selected dates only. Please contact the railway for further details.
Prices: £1.00 per person per ride.
Note: The railway is also available for hire as a venue for childrens parties. Phone (01562) 827232 for further information.

Detailed Directions by Car:
Exit the M5 at Junction 3 and follow the brown tourist signs for the Severn Valley Railway. Alternatively exit the M42 at Junction 1 orthe M5 at Junction 4 and take the A448 from Bromsgrove to Kidderminster before once again following the brown tourist signs for the Severn Valley Railway.

COLNE VALLEY RAILWAY

Address: Castle Hedingham Station, Yeldham Road, Castle Hedingham, Essex, CO9 3DZ
Telephone Nº: (01787) 461174
Year Formed: 1974
Location of Line: On A1017, 7 miles north-west of Braintree
Length of Line: Approximately 1 mile

Nº of Steam Locos: 4
Nº of Other Locos: 11
Nº of Members: 280
Annual Membership Fee: £11.00
Approx Nº of Visitors P.A.: 45,000
Gauge: Standard
Web Site: www.colnevalleyrailway.co.uk

GENERAL INFORMATION

Nearest Mainline Station: Braintree (7 miles)
Nearest Bus Station: Hedingham bus from Braintree stops at the Railway (except on Sundays)
Car Parking: Parking at the site
Coach Parking: Free parking at site
Souvenir Shop(s): Yes
Food & Drinks: Yes – on operational days. Also Pullman Sunday Lunches – bookings necessary.

SPECIAL INFORMATION

The railway is being re-built on a section of the old Colne Valley & Halstead Railway, with all buildings, bridges, signal boxes, etc. re-located on site.
The Railway also has a Farm Park on site which is open from early May until early October.

OPERATING INFORMATION

Opening Times: 2010 dates: Trains run every Sunday and Bank Holiday weekend from 28th March to 3rd October. Open daily in August except for Mondays and Fridays. Pre-booked parties any time by arrangement and various other special events. Please check the web site for further details.
Steam Working: Sundays 10.30pm to 4.00pm, Bank Holidays from 10.30am to 4.00pm and 10.30am to 4.30pm on midweek operating days.
Prices: Adult – Steam days £8.00; Diesel £6.00
       Child – Steam £5.00; Diesel £4.00
       Family (2 adults + 4 children) –
             Steam £28.00; Diesel £22.00
       Senior Citizen – Steam £7.00; Diesel £5.00

Detailed Directions by Car:
The Railway is situated on the A1017 between Halstead and Haverhill, 7 miles north-west of Braintree.

DERBYSHIRE DALES NARROW GAUGE RAILWAY

Correspondence: 44 Midland Terrace, Westhouses, Alfreton   DE55 5AB
Contact Phone Nº: (01629) 580381
Year Formed: 1998
Location of Line: Rowsley South Station, Peak Rail
Length of Line: 500 yards

Nº of Steam Locos: None
Nº of Other Locos: 7
Approx Nº of Visitors P.A.: Not known
Gauge: 2 feet
Web site: www.peakrail.co.uk

GENERAL INFORMATION

Nearest Mainline Station: Matlock (4 miles)
Nearest Bus Station: Matlock (4 miles)
Car Parking: 200 spaces at Rowsley South Station
Coach Parking: Free parking at Rowsley South
Souvenir Shop(s): Yes
Food & Drinks: Yes

SPECIAL INFORMATION

This narrow gauge line is operated at Peak Rail's Rowsley South Station. The line has now been extended to 500 yards.

OPERATING INFORMATION

Opening Times: Sundays and Bank Holiday weekends from April to early October. Also open on certain Wednesdays in July and August – please contact the railway for further information.
Steam Working: None at present.
Prices: Adult £1.00
Children 25p

Detailed Directions by Car:
Follow the A6 Bakewell to Matlock road to Rowsley then follow the brown tourist signs for the Peak Rail Station.

DUNHAM'S WOOD LIGHT RAILWAY

Address: Dunham's Wood, Rodham Road, March   PE15 0DN
Phone Nº: (01760) 338052 (Chairman)
Year Formed: 1989
Location of Line: Just off the B1099 in March, Cambridgeshire
Length of Line: Approximately ½ mile

Nº of Steam Locos: 0
Nº of Other Locos: 8
Nº of Members: Approximately 20
Approx Nº of Visitors P.A.: 1,200
Gauge: 7¼ inches
Web site: www.dunhamswood.co.uk

GENERAL INFORMATION

Nearest Mainline Station: March (3 miles)
Nearest Bus Station: March (2 miles)
Car Parking: Available on site
Coach Parking: Available on site
Food & Drinks: Available on open days

OPERATING INFORMATION

Opening Times: Easter Sunday & Monday, May Bank Holiday Sunday & Monday, Whitsun Sunday & Monday, the last Sunday in July, every Sunday and Bank Holiday in August. Trains run from 2.00pm to 5.00pm.
Steam Working: Only when steam locos visit.
Prices: Adults £1.00
             Children 50p
Note: An extra fee is also charged for entrance to the Wood.

Detailed Directions by Car:
From the A141 North or South, follow directions to March town centre. From here follow the B1099 signposted for Christchurch. After 1 mile cross the railway line then take the next turning on the left into Binnimoor Road. After 1 mile turn right into Rodham Road and the wood is on the left after 200 metres with the Car Park opposite.

EAST ANGLIAN RAILWAY MUSEUM

Address: Chappel & Wakes Colne Station, Colchester, Essex CO6 2DS **Telephone Nº:** (01206) 242524 **Year Formed:** 1969 **Location of Line:** 6 miles west of Colchester on Marks Tey to Sudbury branch **Length of Line:** A third of a mile	**Nº of Steam Locos:** 5 **Other Locos:** 4 **Nº of Members:** 750 **Annual Membership Fee:** Adult £20.00; Senior Citizen £15.00 **Approx Nº of Visitors P.A.:** 40,000 **Gauge:** Standard **Web site:** www.earm.co.uk

GENERAL INFORMATION

Nearest Mainline Station: Chappel & Wakes Colne (adajcent)
Nearest Bus Stop: Chappel (400 yards)
Car Parking: Free parking at site
Coach Parking: Free parking at site
Souvenir Shop(s): Yes
Food & Drinks: Yes – drinks are available every day and snacks are also available on operating days.

SPECIAL INFORMATION

The museum has the most comprehensive collection of railway architecture & engineering in the region. The railway also has a miniature railway that usually operates on steam days.

OPERATING INFORMATION

Opening Times: Open daily 10.00am to 4.30pm. Steam days open from 11.00am to 4.30pm. Closed on Christmas Day and Boxing Day.
Steam Working: Steam days are held every month from April to August and also in October and December. Bank Holidays are also Steam days. Check the web site for further details.
Prices: Adult £4.00 non-Steam; £8.00 Steam
Child £2.00 non-Steam; £4.00 Steam
O.A.P. £3.50 non-Steam; £7.00 Steam
Family £10.00 non-Steam; £20.00 Steam
Children under the age of 4 are admitted free of charge. A 10% discount is available for bookings for more than 10 people. A 10% discount is also available for visitors who visit using Mainline trains!

Detailed Directions by Car:
From North & South: Turn off the A12 south west of Colchester onto the A1124 (formerly the A604). The Museum is situated just off the A1124; From West: Turn off the A120 just before Marks Tey (signposted).

EAST SUFFOLK LIGHT RAILWAY

Address: East Anglia Transport Museum,
Chapel Road, Carlton Colville,
Lowestoft   NR33 8BL
Telephone Nº: (01502) 518459
Year Formed: 1972
Location: 3 miles south of Lowestoft
Length of Line: 200 yards

Nº of Steam Locos: None
Nº of Other Locos: 4
Approx Nº of Visitors P.A.: 18,000
Gauge: 2 feet
Web site: www.eatm.org.uk

GENERAL INFORMATION

Nearest Mainline Station: Oulton Broad South
(2 miles)
Nearest Bus Station: Lowestoft (3 miles)
Car Parking: Available on site
Coach Parking: Available
Souvenir Shop(s): Yes
Food & Drinks: Available

SPECIAL INFORMATION

The railway is located at the East Anglian Transport
Museum which also offers visitors trolleybus and
tram rides.

OPERATING INFORMATION

Opening Times: Sundays and Thursdays from April
to September, also Saturdays from June to
September, Tuesdays and Wednesdays from late July
to the end of August and some other dates. Open
from 2.00pm to 5.00pm on most days but from
11.00am to 5.00pm on Sundays and Bank Holidays.
Steam Working: None
Prices: Adults £6.50 (Admission and all rides)
Children £4.50 (Admission and all rides)
Concessions £5.50 (Admission and rides)

Detailed Directions by Car:
From All Parts: Take the A146 from Lowestoft towards Norwich and turn left onto the B1384 at Carlton Colville.
The Museum and Railway are clearly signposted and are situated just by the side of the B1384.

ECCLESBOURNE VALLEY RAILWAY

Address: Station Road, Coldwell Street, Wirksworth DE4 4FB **Telephone Nº:** (01629) 823076 **Year Formed:** 2000 **Location of Line:** Wirksworth to Duffield **Length of Line:** 4 miles	**Nº of Steam Locos:** 3 **Nº of Other Locos:** 9 **Nº of Members:** 600+ **Annual Membership Fee:** £12.00 **Approx Nº of Visitors P.A.:** 15,000 **Gauge:** Standard **Web site:** www.e-v-r.com

GENERAL INFORMATION

Nearest Mainline Station: Cromford (2 miles)
Nearest Bus Station: Derby (13 miles)
Car Parking: Available at the Station
Coach Parking: Available at the Station
Souvenir Shop(s): Yes
Food & Drinks: Yes

SPECIAL INFORMATION

The line is currently being restored section by section and the Railway now hopes to complete all 8½ miles by 2011.

OPERATING INFORMATION

Opening Times: 2010 dates: Wirksworth to Ravenstor and Idridgehay on weekends and Bank Holidays from 20th March to 31st October. Trains also run from Wirksworth to Ravenstor on Tuesdays, Wednesdays and Thursdays from 27th July to 2nd September. Services usually run from around 11.20am until 3.45pm though times vary. Please contact the railway for further details.
Steam Working: To be introduced in August 2010
Prices: Adult Day Rover £3.50 to £10.00
    Child Day Rover £2.00 to £5.00
    Concessions Day Rover £3.00 to £9.00
    Family Day Rover £10.00 to £18.00
Note: Prices vary depending on journey length.

Detailed Directions by Car:
From All Parts: Exit the M1 at Junction 26 and take the A610 Ambergate then the A6 to Whatstandwell. Turn left onto the B5035 to Wirksworth and the station is at the bottom of the hill as you enter the town.

EVERGREENS MINIATURE RAILWAY

Address: Main Road, Stickney, Boston, Lincolnshire
Telephone Nº: (01205) 723069
Year Formed: 2002
Location of Line: Stickney, off the A16
Length of Line: Over 1,500 metres of 7¼ inch gauge and 400 metres of 5 inch gauge

Nº of Steam Locos: 20
Nº of Other Locos: 15
Nº of Members: 50
Approx Nº of Visitors P.A.: Not known
Gauge: 5 inches and 7¼ inches
Web site: www.evergreensrail.co.uk

GENERAL INFORMATION

Nearest Mainline Station: Boston (10 miles)
Nearest Bus Station: Boston (10 miles)
Car Parking: Available on site
Coach Parking: None
Food & Drinks: Available

SPECIAL INFORMATION

The site of the railway was previously a Horticultural Nursery and is around 3 acres in size. The site currently has 3 level crossings, 3 bridges and 2 ponds and is always undergoing expansion.

OPERATING INFORMATION

Opening Times: The last Saturday of each month from April to October. Trains run from 10.00am to 4.00pm.
Steam Working: Most operating days.
Prices: Admission £2.00 (unlimited rides)

Detailed Directions by Car:
The railway is situated on the A16 between Boston and Spilsby. Upon reaching the village of Stickney, look out for the signal on the grass verge which marks the entrance to the railway.

EVESHAM VALE LIGHT RAILWAY

Address: Evesham Country Park, Twyford, Evesham WR11 4TP	**Nº of Steam Locos:** 6
Telephone Nº: (01386) 422282	**Nº of Other Locos:** 3
Year Formed: 2002	**Approx Nº of Visitors P.A.:** 50,000
Location of Line: 1 mile north of Evesham	**Gauge:** 15 inches
Length of Line: 1¼ miles	**Web site:** www.evlr.co.uk

GENERAL INFORMATION

Nearest Mainline Station: Evesham (1 mile)
Nearest Bus Station: Evesham (1½ miles)
Car Parking: Available in the Country Park
Coach Parking: Available in the Country Park
Souvenir Shop(s): Yes
Food & Drinks: Restaurant at the Garden Centre

SPECIAL INFORMATION

The railway is situated within the 130 acre Evesham Country Park which has apple orchards and picnic areas overlooking the picturesque Vale of Evesham.

OPERATING INFORMATION

Opening Times: Open at weekends throughout the year and daily during school holidays. Trains run from 10.30am to 5.00pm (until 4.00pm during the winter). Please phone for further details.
Steam Working: Daily when trains are running.
Prices: Adult Return £2.00
Child Return £1.40
Senior Citizen Return £1.70

Detailed Directions by Car:
From the North: Exit the M42 at Junction 3 and take the A435 towards Alcester then the A46 to Evesham; From the South: Exit the M5 at Junction 9 and take the A46 to Evesham; From the West: Exit the M5 at Junction 7 and take the A44 to Evesham; From the East: Take the A44 from Oxford to Evesham. Upon reaching Evesham, follow the Brown tourist signs for Evesham Country Park and the railway.

FENLAND LIGHT RAILWAY

Address: Mereside Farm, Mereside Drove, Ramsey Mereside, Cambs.	**N° of Steam Locos**: 3+
	N° of Other Locos: 2+
Telephone N°: None	**N° of Members**: 12
Year Formed: 1991	**Approx N° of Visitors P.A.**: 500 – 1,000
Location of Line: Mereside Farm	**Gauge**: 7¼ inches
Length of Line: 800 feet	**Web site**: www.fenlandlightrailway.co.uk

GENERAL INFORMATION

Nearest Mainline Station: Peterborough (10 miles)
Nearest Bus Station: Peterborough (10 miles)
Car Parking: Available on site
Coach Parking: None
Food & Drinks: Available

SPECIAL INFORMATION

The railway is operated by volunteers from the Ramsey Miniature Steam Railway Society.

OPERATING INFORMATION

Opening Times: The third Sunday of each month from April to October inclusive except for August when two days are spent at the nearby RAF Upwood fair. There are also two Santa Special running days near to the Christmas holidays and at least two other charity running days when proceeds go to a local charity.
Steam Working: All operating days.
Prices: £1.00 per ride

Detailed Directions by Car:
From Ramsey: Travel up Great Whyte, turn right at the mini-roundabout by the Mill Apartments and follow onto Stocking Fen Road. Follow this road for just over a mile then turn left into Bodsey Toll Road for Ramsey Mereside. Follow this road until the signpost for Ramsey Mereside and turn right into Mereside Drove. The railway is on the left after approximately 1 mile.

FERRY MEADOWS MINIATURE RAILWAY

Address: Ham Lane, Nene Park,
Oundle Road, Peterborough PE2 5UU
Telephone Nº: (01933) 398889
Year Formed: 1978
Location of Line: Nene Leisure Park
Length of Line: 700 yards

Nº of Steam Locos: Guest locos only
Nº of Other Locos: 2
Approx Nº of Visitors P.A.: Not known
Gauge: 10¼ inches
Web site: www.ferrymeadowsrailway.co.uk

GENERAL INFORMATION

Nearest Mainline Station: Peterborough (2 miles)
Nearest Bus Station: Peterborough (2 miles)
Car Parking: Available adjacent
Coach Parking: Available adjacent
Souvenir Shop(s): Yes
Food & Drinks: Available

SPECIAL INFORMATION

The railway is situated in the Ferry Meadows area of
Nene Park in which watersports and other leisure
activities are also available.

OPERATING INFORMATION

Opening Times: 2010 dates: Every weekend from
13th March to 31st October and daily during the
school holidays (though closed on Mondays).
Trains run from 11.30am to 4.30pm.
Steam Working: Bank Holidays and weekends in
August when guest steam locomotives operate.
Prices: Adult Return £2.50
    Child Return £1.50

Detailed Directions by Car:
Nene Park is situated on the A605 Oundle Road. Follow the brown tourist signs for Nene Valley Park.

FOXFIELD STEAM RAILWAY

Address: Caverswall Road Station, Blythe Bridge, Stoke-on-Trent, Staffs. ST11 9EA	**Nº of Steam Locos**: 22
Telephone Nº: (01782) 396210	**Nº of Other Locos**: 15
Year Formed: 1967	**Nº of Members**: Over 300
Location of Line: Blythe Bridge	**Annual Membership Fee**: Adult £12.00; Junior £6.00; Family £20.00
Length of Line: 3½ miles	**Approx Nº of Visitors P.A.**: 25,000
Gauge: Standard	**Web site**: www.foxfieldrailway.co.uk

GENERAL INFORMATION

Nearest Mainline Station: Blythe Bridge (¼ mile)
Nearest Bus Station: Hanley (5 miles)
Car Parking: Space for 300 cars available
Coach Parking: Space for 6 coaches available
Souvenir Shop(s): Yes
Food & Drinks: Yes – Buffet and Real Ale Bar

SPECIAL INFORMATION

The Railway is a former Colliery railway built in 1893 to take coal from Foxfield Colliery. It has the steepest Standard Gauge adhesion worked gradient in the UK and freight trains can be seen on these gradients during the annual Steam Gala in July.

OPERATING INFORMATION

Opening Times: Sundays & Bank Holiday Mondays from Easter to the end of October. Also weekends in December. Open 11.00am to 5.00pm.
Steam Working: 11.30am, 1.00pm, 2.30pm and 4.00pm although Special Event days also run trains at earlier times.
Prices: Adult Tickets – £7.50
Child Tickets – £3.00 (3-16 years old)
Senior Citizen Tickets – £5.50
Fares may vary on special event days.

Detailed Directions by Car:

From South: Exit M6 at Junction 14 onto the A34 to Stone then the A520 to Meir and the A50 to Blythe Bridge; From North: Exit M6 at Junction 15 then the A500 to Stoke-on-Trent and the A50 to Blythe Bridge; From East: Take the A50 to Blythe Bridge. Once in Blythe Bridge, turn by the Mainline crossing.

GOLDEN VALLEY LIGHT RAILWAY

Address: Butterley Station, Ripley, Derbyshire DE5 3QZ	**N° of Steam Locos**: 2
Telephone N°: (01773) 747674	**N° of Other Locos**: 17
Year Formed: 1987	**N° of Members**: 75
Location of Line: Butterley, near Ripley	**Annual Membership Fee**: £16.00
Length of Line: Four-fifths of a mile	**Approx N° of Visitors P.A.**: 10,000
Web site: www.gvlr.org.uk	**Gauge**: 2 feet

GENERAL INFORMATION

Nearest Mainline Station: Alfreton (6 miles)
Nearest Bus Station: Bus stop outside the Station
Car Parking: Free parking at site – ample space
Coach Parking: Free parking at site
Souvenir Shop(s): Yes – at Butterley and Swanwick
Food & Drinks: Yes – both sites

SPECIAL INFORMATION

The Golden Valley Light Railway is part of the Midland Railway – Butterley and runs from the museum site through the country park to Newlands Inn Station close to the Cromford Canal and the pub of the same name.

OPERATING INFORMATION

Opening Times: 2010 dates: Weekends and Bank Holidays from April to October and daily from 1st to 11th April, 31st May to 6th June and 24th July to 5th September. Trains run from 11.45am to 4.15pm.
Steam Working: One weekend per month – please contact the railway for further details.
Prices: Adult £2.00
　　　　　Children £1.00

Detailed Directions by Car:
From All Parts: From the M1 exit at Junction 28 and take the A38 towards Derby. The Centre is signposted at the junction with the B6179.

Great Central Railway

Address: Great Central Station, Great Central Road, Loughborough, Leicestershire LE11 1RW **Telephone Nº**: (01509) 230726 **Year Formed**: 1969 **Location of Line**: From Loughborough to Leicester	**Length of Line**: 8 miles **Nº of Steam Locos**: 10 **Nº of Other Locos**: 11 **Nº of Members**: 5,000 **Annual Membership Fee**: £25.00 **Approx Nº of Visitors P.A.**: 150,000 **Gauge**: Standard

GENERAL INFORMATION

Nearest Mainline Station: Loughborough (1 mile)
Nearest Bus Station: Loughborough (½ mile)
Car Parking: Street parking outside the Station
Coach Parking: Car parks at Quorn & Woodhouse, Rothley and Leicester North
Souvenir Shop(s): Yes
Food & Drinks: Yes – Buffet or Restaurant cars are usually available for snacks or other meals

Web site: www.gcrailway.co.uk

SPECIAL INFORMATION

The aim of the GCR is to recreate the experience of British main line railway operation during the best years of steam locomotives.

OPERATING INFORMATION

Opening Times: 2010 dates: Weekends throughout the year, most Wednesdays in July then Tuesday to Thursday 20th July to 2nd September. Santa Specials in December.
Steam Working: Weekends, Bank Holidays and some Special Events throughout the year.
Prices: Adult Day ticket £14.00
Child Day ticket £9.00
Senior Citizen Day ticket £12.00
Family Day Ticket £32 (2 adults + 3 children)

Detailed Directions by Car:
Great Central Road is on the South East side of Loughborough and is clearly signposted from the A6 Leicester Road and A60 Nottingham Road.

GREAT CENTRAL RAILWAY (NOTTINGHAM)

Address: Nottingham Transport Heritage Centre, Mere Way, Ruddington, Nottingham NG11 6NX	**Length of Line:** 9 miles
	N° of Steam Locos: 6
	N° of Other Locos: 10
Telephone N°: (0115) 940-5705	**N° of Members:** 750
Fax N°: (0115) 940-5905	**Annual Membership Fee:** £14.00
Year Formed: 1990 (Opened in 1994)	**Approx N° of Visitors P.A.:** 15,000
Location of Line: Ruddington to Loughborough Junction	**Gauge:** Standard
	Web site: www.nthc.co.uk

GENERAL INFORMATION

Nearest Mainline Station: Nottingham (5 miles)
Nearest Bus Station: Bus service from Nottingham to Ruddington
Car Parking: Free parking at site
Coach Parking: Free parking at site
Souvenir Shop(s): Yes
Food & Drinks: Yes

SPECIAL INFORMATION

The Heritage Centre covers an area of over eleven acres and is set within the Rushcliffe Country Park in Ruddington. Trains run to Loughborough Junction or Rushcliffe Halt.

OPERATING INFORMATION

Opening Times: Sundays and Bank Holidays plus some Saturdays from Easter until October. Open 10.45am to 5.00pm. Also open for Santa Specials on December weekends.
Steam Working: Steam service runs from 11.30am
Prices: Adult   £6.50 – £8.00
          Child   £3.50 – £4.00
          Senior Citizens £5.50 – £7.00
          Family   £18.50 – £22.00
             (2 adults + 2 children)
Note: Prices vary depending on the journey length.

Detailed Directions by Car:
From All Parts: The centre is situated off the A60 Nottingham to Loughborough Road and is signposted just south of the traffic lights at Ruddington.

GREAT WOBURN RAILWAY

Address: Woburn Safari Park MK17 9QN
Telephone Nº: (01525) 290407
Year Formed: 1970
Location of Line: Near Milton Keynes
Length of Line: 1½ miles

Nº of Steam Locos: None
Nº of Other Locos: 3
Approx Nº of Visitors P.A.: Over 420,000 (to the Park)
Gauge: 2 feet 6 inches
Web site: www.woburn.co.uk

GENERAL INFORMATION

Nearest Mainline Station: Ridgmont (1½ miles)
Nearest Tube Station: Milton Keynes (11 miles)
Car Parking: Available on site
Coach Parking: Available on site
Souvenir Shop(s): Yes
Food & Drinks: Available

SPECIAL INFORMATION

The railway runs around Woburn Safari Park which also houses a number of other attractions.

OPERATING INFORMATION

Opening Times: Daily from the beginning of March to the end of October from 10.00am to 5.00pm. Weekends only from mid-November to the end of February, 11.00am to 3.00pm.
Steam Working: None
Prices: Adults £18.50 (Admission to the park)
Children £13.50 (Admission to the park)
Concessions £15.50 (Admission to park)
Family £52.00 (Admission to the park)
Note: Prices are reduced during the Winter months.

Detailed Directions by Car:
From All Parts: Exit the M1 at Junction 13 and take the A507 then the A4012 to Woburn Safari Park which is clearly signposted.

GRIMSBY & CLEETHORPES M.E.S.

Address: Waltham Windmill, Brigsley Road, Waltham, Grimsby DN32 0JZ
Telephone N°: None
Year Formed: 1985
Location: Waltham, near Grimsby
Length of Line: 1,300 feet for 7¼ and 5 inch gauges, 600 feet for 3½ gauge

N° of Steam Locos: 1
N° of Other Locos: 1
N° of Members: Approximately 80
Approx N° of Visitors P.A.: Not known
Gauge: 3½ inches, 5 inches & 7¼ inches
Web site: www.gcmes.org.uk

GENERAL INFORMATION

Nearest Mainline Station: Grimsby (3 miles)
Nearest Bus Station: Grimsby (3 miles)
Car Parking: Available on site
Coach Parking: None
Food & Drinks: Available at the Windmill

SPECIAL INFORMATION

The Society's track is based in Waltham, near Grimsby adjacent to a preserved windmill dating back to 1878 which still operates from time to time.

OPERATING INFORMATION

Opening Times: Sundays and Bank Holidays from April to September inclusive. Trains run from 1.00pm to 4.00pm.
Steam Working: Most operating days.
Prices: 50p per ride.

Detailed Directions by Car:
The Railway is situated by Waltham Windmill on the B1203 Grimsby to Binbrook Road and is well signposted. The B1203 connects to the A16 at Scartho, a suburb of Grimsby, about a mile from the railway or to the A18 at Ashby Top, about 3 miles away.

HALL LEYS MINIATURE RAILWAY

Address: Hall Leys Park, Matlock, Derbyshire
Telephone Nº: 07525 217116
Year Formed: 1948
Location of Line: Hall Leys Park
Length of Line: 200 yards

Nº of Steam Locos: None
Nº of Other Locos: 1
Approx Nº of Visitors P.A.: Not known
Gauge: 9½ inches

GENERAL INFORMATION

Nearest Mainline Station: Matlock (½ mile)
Nearest Bus Station: Matlock (by the train station)
Car Parking: Available near the train station on the new bypass
Coach Parking: As above

SPECIAL INFORMATION

The Hall Leys Miniature Railway has operated in Matlock since 1948 and is one of only 4 railways in the country to run a line with the unusual 9½ inch gauge. The park hosts a number of other attractions including a children's playground with a paddling pool, a lake with motor boats, a skate park and bowling and putting greens.

OPERATING INFORMATION

Opening Times: Weekends from mid-March to the end of September and daily during the school holidays in this period.
Steam Working: None at present.
Prices: 60p per ride.

Detailed Directions by Car:
Hall Leys Park is situated in the centre of Matlock between the River Derwent and the A615 Causeway Lane.

HILCOTE VALLEY RAILWAY

Address: Fletchers Garden Centre, Bridge Farm, Stone Road, Eccleshall, ST21 6JY	**Nᵒ of Steam Locos**: 3
Telephone Nᵒ: (01785) 284553	**Nᵒ of Other Locos**: 2
Year Formed: 1993	**Nᵒ of Members**: –
Location of Line: Eccleshall, Staffordshire	**Approx Nᵒ of Visitors P.A.**: 5,000+
Length of Line: 500 yards	**Gauge**: 7¼ inches
	Web site: www.freewebs.com/hilcotevalleyrailway/

GENERAL INFORMATION

Nearest Mainline Station: Stafford (6 miles)
Nearest Bus Station: Stafford (6 miles)
Car Parking: Available on site
Coach Parking: Available
Souvenir Shop(s): None
Food & Drinks: Available on site

SPECIAL INFORMATION

Railway enthusiast Roger Greatrex designed and built this railway himself!

OPERATING INFORMATION

Opening Times: Weekends and Bank Holidays from Good Friday to the end of October from 11.30am to 5.00pm. Also open on afternoons during the School Holidays, 1.30pm to 4.30pm.
Steam Working: Sundays only.
Prices: Adults £1.00
Children £1.00

Detailed Directions by Car:
From All Parts: Exit the M6 at Junction 14 and take the A5013 to Eccleshall. Just after the junction with the A519, turn right onto the B5026 Stone Road and the Garden Centre is on the right at Bridge Farm after ¾ mile.

HOLLYBUSH MINIATURE RAILWAY

Address: Hollybush Garden Centre, Warstone Road, Shareshill, Wolverhampton   WV10 7LX
Telephone Nº: (01922) 418050
Year Formed: 1996
Location of Line: Wolverhampton
Length of Line: 950 yards

Nº of Steam Locos: None
Nº of Other Locos: 2
Nº of Members: –
Approx Nº of Visitors P.A.: Not known
Gauge: 7¼ inches
Web site: www.hollybush-garden.com/miniature-railway/

GENERAL INFORMATION

Nearest Mainline Station: Cannock (4 miles)
Nearest Bus Station: Cannock (4 miles)
Car Parking: Available on site
Coach Parking: Available
Souvenir Shop(s): Yes
Food & Drinks: Available

OPERATING INFORMATION

Opening Times: Wednesday to Sunday from Easter to early September and daily during the School Holidays. Also weekends from September to Christmas. Trains run from 10.30am to 4.30pm.
Steam Working: None at present.
Prices: Adults £1.50
　　　　　 Children £1.50

Detailed Directions by Car:
From All Parts: Exit the M6 at Junction 11 and follow the brown tourist signs onto the A462 for the railway which is on the left after approximately 600 yards.

KING'S LYNN & DISTRICT S.M.E.

Address: Lynnsport, Green Park Avenue, King's Lynn, Norfolk PE30 2NB
Telephone N°: (01366) 381182
Year Formed: 1972
Location of Line: King's Lynn
Length of Line: 627 feet

N° of Steam Locos: 6
N° of Other Locos: 11
N° of Members: 52
Annual Membership Fee: £17.00 Adult
Approx N° of Visitors P.A.: 1,200
Gauge: 3½ inches, 5 inches & 7¼ inches
Web site: www.kldsme.org.uk

GENERAL INFORMATION

Nearest Mainline Station: King's Lynn (1 mile)
Nearest Bus Station: King's Lynn (1 mile)
Car Parking: Available on site
Coach Parking: Available
Food & Drinks: Available in Lynnsport

SPECIAL INFORMATION

The King's Lynn & District Society of Model Engineers first operated a railway in 1972 and the current track at Lynnsport has been working since 1992. Improvements to the Lynnsport facilities have been ongoing ever since.

OPERATING INFORMATION

Opening Times: Every Sunday from Easter until the end of October. Trains run from 12.00pm to 5.00pm
Steam Working: Most operating days.
Prices: 50p per ride.

Detailed Directions by Car:
Lynnsport is well-signposted from the outskirts of King's Lynn so it is easy to find just by following the signs. The railway itself is signposted once in the Lynnsport car park.

KINVER & WEST MIDLANDS S.M.E.

Correspondence: 24 Goodrest Avenue, Halesowen, West Midlands   B62 0HP
Telephone Nº: (0121) 602-2019
Year Formed: 1961
Location of Line: Marsh Playing Fields, Kinver, Staffordshire
Length of Line: ½ mile

Nº of Steam Locos: Members locos only
Nº of Other Locos: Members locos only
Nº of Members: Approximately 100
Approx Nº of Visitors P.A.: Not known
Gauge: 3½ inches and 5 inches
Website: www.kinvermodelengineers.org.uk

GENERAL INFORMATION

Nearest Mainline Station: Kidderminster (6 miles)
Nearest Bus Station: Stourbridge (3 miles)
Car Parking: Available on site
Coach Parking: Available on site
Food & Drinks: None

SPECIAL INFORMATION

The Kinver & West Midlands Society of Model Engineers dates back to organisations formed in the 1920s and has operated a railway in Kinver since 1962. In addition to the main 3½ and 5 inch line, a short 7¼ inch track is now in operation at the site.

OPERATING INFORMATION

Opening Times: Sunday afternoons between Easter and October, weather permitting. Trains run between 2.00pm and 5.00pm.
Steam Working: Most operating days.
Prices: £1.00 per ride.

Detailed Directions by Car:
The Society's tracksite is situated on the Marsh Playing Fields at the end of the High Street in the village of Kinver which is to the West of Stourbridge and to the North of Kidderminster.

LAVENDON NARROW GAUGE RAILWAY

Address: 8 Harrold Road, Lavendon, Olney MK46 4HU
Telephone Nº: (01234) 712653
Year Formed: 1990
Location of Line: Lavendon, Bucks
Length of Line: 500 yards

Nº of Steam Locos: 1
Nº of Other Locos: 2
Nº of Members: –
Approx Nº of Visitors P.A.: 3,000
Gauge: 7¼ inches
Web site: www.lavendonconnection.com/LNGR.htm

GENERAL INFORMATION

Nearest Mainline Station: Milton Keynes (12 miles)
Nearest Bus Station: Milton Keynes (12 miles)
Car Parking: Available on site
Coach Parking: None
Souvenir Shop(s): None
Food & Drinks: Available

SPECIAL INFORMATION

The Lavendon Narrow Gauge Railway is located in the grounds of the owner's home and raises funds for local charities.

OPERATING INFORMATION

Opening Times: 2010 dates: 18th April, 16th May, 13th June, 11th July, 12th September and 10th October. Trains run from 11.00am to 5.00pm. Bookings are necessary for the Santa Specials which run from 12th to 18th December.
Steam Working: Normally diesel operation. Please contact the railway for details about steam working.
Prices: Adults £1.00
           Children £1.00
Note: Higher fares are charged for special events.

Detailed Directions by Car:
From All Parts: Lavendon is situated on the A428 Bedford to Northampton road and the railway's location is signposted from the main road on operating days.

LEASOWES MINIATURE RAILWAY

Address: Leasowes Park, Mucklow Hill, Halesowen   B62 8QF
Telephone Nº: (01562) 710614
Year Formed: 1990
Location: Halesowen, West Midlands
Length of Line: 400 yards

Nº of Steam Locos: 1
Nº of Other Locos: 1
Nº of Members: –
Approx Nº of Visitors P.A.: 4,000
Gauge: 7¼ inches
Web site: None

GENERAL INFORMATION

Nearest Mainline Station: Old Hill (3 miles)
Nearest Bus Station: Halesowen (1 mile)
Car Parking: Available on site
Coach Parking: Available
Souvenir Shop(s): None
Food & Drinks: Due to be available in 2010.

SPECIAL INFORMATION

At the time of going to press, the Leasowes Miniature Railway was not in operation due to some damage to the line caused by construction work on a nearby canal. However, it is hoped that the railway will be operational once again later in 2010. Please contact the railway for further details.

OPERATING INFORMATION

Opening Times: Sunday afternoons throughout the year from 2.30pm to 5.00pm (open until 6.30pm during the Summer)
Steam Working: Most operating days.
Prices: 50p per ride

Detailed Directions by Car:
From All Parts: Exit the M5 at Junction 3 and take the A456 towards Halesowen. Turn right onto the A459 at the roundabout and continue to the next roundabout and take the 3rd exit, following signs for Mucklow Hill. The railway is on the right after about ¼ mile and is clearly signposted 'Leasowes Park'.

LEICESTER SOCIETY OF MODEL ENGINEERS

Address: Abbey Park, Leicester LE1 3EJ
Telephone Nº: (01455) 272047
Year Formed: 1909
Location of Line: Victorian Public Park
Length of Line: 500 yards

Nº of Steam Locos: 10+
Nº of Other Locos: 5
Nº of Members: 100+
Annual Membership Fee: –
Approx Nº of Visitors P.A.: 5,000+
Gauges: 3½ inches, 5 inches & 7¼ inches
Web site: www.lsme.org.uk

GENERAL INFORMATION

Nearest Mainline Station: Leicester (1½ miles)
Nearest Bus Station: Leicester (½ mile)
Car Parking: Available on site
Coach Parking: None
Souvenir Shop(s): None
Food & Drinks: None, but available elsewhere in the Park

SPECIAL INFORMATION

The Society celebrated it's Centenary in 2009 and has been located at Abbey Park since 1953.

OPERATING INFORMATION

Opening Times: Sundays, Bank Holidays and occasional Saturdays from Easter until the end of October. Trains run from 2.00pm to 5.00pm.
Steam Working: Most operating days.
Prices: Adults £1.00
Children £1.00 (Under-5s ride for free)
Family Ticket £3.00 (2 adults + 3 children)

Detailed Directions by Car:
From All Parts: The railway is located at the South-Western edge of Leicester's Abbey Park. Take the inner ring road to St. Margaret's Bus Station and vehicular access to the park is by the nearby Slater Street entrance (off St.Margaret's Way).

LINCOLNSHIRE COAST LIGHT RAILWAY

Address: Skegness Water Leisure Park,
Walls Lane, Skegness   PE25 1JF
Telephone Nº: (01754) 897400
Year Formed: 1960 (re-opened in 2009)
Location of Line: Skegness
Length of Line: ¾ miles
Nº of Steam Locos: 1 awaiting restoration

Nº of Other Locos: 4
Nº of Members: Approximately 50
Approx Nº of Visitors P.A.: 5,000
Gauge: 2 feet
Web site:
www.lincolnshire-coast-light-railway.co.uk

GENERAL INFORMATION

Nearest Mainline Station: Skegness (3 miles)
Nearest Bus Station: Skegness (3 miles)
Car Parking: Free parking available on site
Coach Parking: Free parking available on site
Souvenir Shop(s): None
Food & Drinks: Available

SPECIAL INFORMATION

The railway was originally located some distance up
the coast at the Cleethorpes/Humberston 'Fitties'
before closure during the 1980s.

OPERATING INFORMATION

Opening Times: 2010 dates: 3rd, 30th & 31st May;
18th & 25th July; 1st, 8th, 15th, 22nd, 29th & 30th
August and a Gala weekend on 4th & 5th September.
Steam Working: Please contact the railway for
further details.
Prices: Adults £1.00
            Children £1.00

Detailed Directions by Car:
From All Parts: Take the A52 North from Skegness (signposted for Ingoldmells) and continue for 3 miles. Turn
left onto Walls Lane opposite the Butlins signposted for the Water Leisure Park. After ¼ mile turn left into the
Park and follow the signs for the Railway.

LINCOLNSHIRE WOLDS RAILWAY

Address: The Railway Station, Ludborough, Lincolnshire DN36 5SQ
Telephone Nº: (01507) 363881
Year Formed: 1979
Location of Line: Ludborough – off the A16(T) between Grimsby and Louth
Length of Line: 1½ miles

Nº of Steam Locos: 3　**Other Locos:** 7
Nº of Members of the Supporting Society (LWRS): 400+
Annual Membership Fee: £26.00 Family, £13.00 Adult, £8.00 Senior Citizen
Approx Nº of Visitors P.A.: 9,000
Gauge: Standard

Photo courtesy of B. Wakefield

GENERAL INFORMATION

Nearest Mainline Station: Grimsby (8 miles)
Nearest Bus Stop: Ludborough (½ mile)
Car Parking: Available at Ludborough Station only
Coach Parking: Space for 1 coach only
Souvenir Shop(s): Yes
Food & Drinks: Yes

SPECIAL INFORMATION

The buildings and facilities at Ludborough have been completed and short steam trips commenced in 1998. A line extension to North Thoresby (1½ miles) is now open.

OPERATING INFORMATION

Opening Times: Certain Sundays from January to December, Wednesdays in August and Santa Specials in December. Please note that advance bookings are essential for Santa Specials.
Steam Working: Contact the Railway for details.
Prices: Adults £6.00　　Children £3.00
　　　　　　Senior Citizens £4.00
　　　　　　Family £15.00 (2 adults + 4 children)
Different fares may apply at Special Events.
Prices include unlimited rides throughout the day.

Web site: www.lincolnshirewoldsrailway.co.uk

Detailed Directions by Car:
The Railway is situated near Ludborough, ½ mile off the A16(T) Louth to Grimsby road. Follow signs to Fulstow to reach the station (approximately ½ mile). Do not turn into Ludborough but stay on the bypass.

LITTLE HAY MINIATURE RAILWAY

Address: Balleny Green, Little Hay Lane, Little Hay   WS14 0QA
Telephone Nº: (01543) 683729
Fax Nº: (01543) 674779
Year Formed: 1948
Location of Line: To the North of Little Hay Hamlet
Length of Line: One third of a mile

Nº of Steam Locos: 20 (approximately)
Nº of Other Locos: 4
Nº of Members: Approximately 120
Approx Nº of Visitors P.A.: 4,500
Gauge: 2½ inches, 3½ inches, 5 inches and 7¼ inches
Web site: www.scmes.co.uk

GENERAL INFORMATION

Nearest Mainline Station: Blake Street (1½ miles)
Nearest Bus Station: Sutton Coldfield or Lichfield (each approximately 5 miles)
Car Parking: Available on site
Coach Parking: None
Food & Drinks: Drinks available at all times with food available at some special events

SPECIAL INFORMATION

The Railway is operated by members of the Sutton Coldfield Model Engineering Society and has been based at Balleny Green since 1981. The site has been progressively developed since this date.

OPERATING INFORMATION

Opening Times: Some Saturdays, Sundays and Bank Holidays throughout the year. Also at various other dates. Please contact the Society or check their web site for further details.
Steam Working: All operating days.
Prices: Prices depend on the event being held.

Detailed Directions by Car:
From the A38/A5 Junction: Head south on the A38 dual carriageway and turn right at the sign for Little Hay. Follow the road past the Pumping Station and after ¼ mile turn left through the steel gates set in stone columns with lanterns to enter the railway. Continue over the level crossing and turn right for the car park.

MABLETHORPE MINIATURE RAILWAY

Address: Queens Park, Mablethorpe, LN12 2AS
Telephone Nº: 07946 499750
Year Formed: 1968
Location: Mablethorpe, Lincolnshire
Length of Line: 200 yards

Nº of Steam Locos: None
Nº of Other Locos: 1
Approx Nº of Visitors P.A.: 12,000
Gauge: 7¼ inches
Web site: None

GENERAL INFORMATION

Nearest Mainline Station: Skegness (17 miles)
Nearest Bus Station: Skegness (17 miles)
Car Parking: Available on site
Coach Parking: Available
Souvenir Shop(s): None
Food & Drinks: Available in the Park

OPERATING INFORMATION

Opening Times: Daily from Easter until the end of October, weather and maintenance permitting. Trains run from 10.00am to 4.00pm.
Steam Working: None
Prices: Adults £1.00
    Children £1.00

Detailed Directions by Car:
From All Parts: Take the A1104 or A52 to Mablethorpe and Queens Park is located on the A52 adjacent to the beach and near to the Eagle Hotel.

MANOR PARK MINIATURE RAILWAY

Address: Manor Park Road, Glossop, SK13 7SH
Telephone Nº: 07779 601180
Year Formed: 1970
Location of Line: Glossop, Derbyshire
Length of Line: 1,164 yards

Nº of Steam Locos: Visiting locos only
Nº of Other Locos: 6
Nº of Members: –
Approx Nº of Visitors P.A.: 13,500
Gauge: 7¼ inches
Web site: None

Regrettably, no suitable photograph of the railway was available at the time of going to press.

GENERAL INFORMATION

Nearest Mainline Station: Glossop (¼ mile)
Nearest Bus Station: Manchester (17 miles)
Car Parking: Available on site
Coach Parking: None
Souvenir Shop(s): None
Food & Drinks: Available in the Park

OPERATING INFORMATION

Opening Times: Weekends and daily during the School Holidays from April until the end of September. Trains run from 11.00am to 4.00pm.
Steam Working: Visiting engines only. Please contact the railway for further information.
Prices: Adults £1.50
Children £1.50
Day Rover Tickets £2.00

Detailed Directions by Car:
From All Parts: The Park is located by the side of the A57 in Glossop and can be easily found by following the brown tourist signs.

MARKEATON PARK LIGHT RAILWAY

Address: Markeaton Park, Derby, DE22
Telephone Nº: (01623) 552292
Year Formed: 1989
Location of Line: Markeaton Park
Length of Line: 1,400 yards
Web site: http://markeaton-park-light-railway.webs.com

Nº of Steam Locos: None
Nº of Other Locos: 2
Approx Nº of Visitors P.A.: Not known
Gauge: 15 inches

GENERAL INFORMATION

Nearest Mainline Station: Derby (2 miles)
Nearest Bus Station: Derby (2 miles)
Car Parking: Available adjacent to the railway
Coach Parking: Available
Souvenir Shop(s): None
Food & Drinks: Available

SPECIAL INFORMATION

Markeaton Park Light Railway opened in 1989 and after extensions in 1996 now runs from the main car park, over two major bridges to a second terminus adjacent to the play area at Mundy Halt.

OPERATING INFORMATION

Opening Times: During weekends and school holidays throughout the year with trains running hourly from 11.00am to 6.30pm during summer months and until 4.00pm during winter months.
Steam Working: None at present. Steam may return in the shape of visiting locomotives, namely the former resident engine , 'Markeaton Lady'.
Prices: Single £1.00   Return £2.00

Detailed Directions by Car:
Markeaton Park is situated in the North-West corner of Derby just to the North of the Junction between the A38 Queensway and A52 Ashbourne Road. The railway itself is situated adjacent to the main car park.

MELTON MOWBRAY MINIATURE RAILWAY

Address: Wilton Park, Leicester Road Sports Ground, Melton Mowbray, LE13 0BG
Telephone N°: (01664) 564559
Year Formed: 1975
Location of Line:
Length of Line: 500 yards

N° of Steam Locos: None
N° of Other Locos: 1
N° of Members: –
Approx N° of Visitors P.A.: Not known
Gauge: 10¼ inches
Web site: None

Regrettably, no suitable photograph of the railway was available at the time of going to press.

GENERAL INFORMATION

Nearest Mainline Station: Melton Mowbray (¼ mile)
Nearest Bus Station: Melton Mowbray (¼ mile)
Car Parking: Available on site
Coach Parking: Available
Souvenir Shop(s): None
Food & Drinks: Available

SPECIAL INFORMATION

The railway is located in Wilton Park, one of the town centre parks which is owned and operated by the Melton Mowbray Town Estate, a charitable trust which was established in 1549.

OPERATING INFORMATION

Opening Times: Daily from Easter to October, weather permitting. Trains run from 10.00am to 4.00pm.
Steam Working: None
Prices: Adults £1.50
Children £1.50

Detailed Directions by Car:
From All Parts: Take the A606 or A607 to Melton Mowbray. The Park is situated to the south of the A607 Leicester Road near to the Melton Mowbray swimming baths.

MIDLAND RAILWAY – BUTTERLEY

Address: Butterley Station, Ripley, Derbyshire DE5 3QZ	**No of Steam Locos**: 22 (+53 Other Locos)
Telephone No: (01773) 747674	**No of Members**: 2,000
Year Formed: 1969	**Annual Membership Fee**: £16.00
Location of Line: Butterley, near Ripley	**Approx No of Visitors P.A.**: 130,000
Length of Line: Standard gauge 3½ miles, Narrow gauge 0.8 mile	**Gauge**: Standard, various Narrow gauges and miniature
	Web: www.midlandrailwaycentre.co.uk

GENERAL INFORMATION

Nearest Mainline Station: Alfreton (6 miles)
Nearest Bus Station: Bus stop outside Butterley Station.
Car Parking: Free parking at site – ample space
Coach Parking: Free parking at site
Souvenir Shop(s): Yes – at Butterley and Swanwick
Food & Drinks: Yes – both sites + bar on train

SPECIAL INFORMATION

The Centre is a unique project with a huge Museum development together with narrow gauge, miniature & model railways as well as a country park and farm park. Includes an Award-winning Victorian Railwayman's church and Princess Royal Class Locomotive Trust Depot.

OPERATING INFORMATION

Opening Times: Open daily throughout the year (closed on Christmas Day and Boxing Day) – trains do not run every day it is open however.
Steam Working: Weekends and bank holidays throughout the year and most days in the school holidays. Phone for further details. 'Day Out With Thomas' 2010 events: 29th May to 2nd June; 4th to 8th August; 27th to 31st December.
Prices: Adult £10.95
　　　　　Children £5.50
　　　　　Senior Citizens £9.95
　　　　　Family £29.70 (2 adults + 3 children)
Note: Some special events are more expensive.

Detailed Directions by Car:
From All Parts: From the M1 exit at Junction 28 and take the A38 towards Derby. The Centre is signposted at the junction with the B6179.

MID-NORFOLK RAILWAY

Address: The Railway Station, Station Road, Dereham NR19 1DF	**Nº of Steam Locos:** Visiting locos only
Telephone Nº: (01362) 690633 or 851723	**Nº of Other Locos:** 8
Year Formed: 1995	**Nº of Members:** 1,000
Location: East Dereham to Wymondham	**Annual Membership Fee:** £16.00
Length of Line: 11 miles	**Approx Nº of Visitors P.A.:** 16,000
	Gauge: Standard
	Web site: www.mnr.org.uk

GENERAL INFORMATION

Nearest Mainline Station: Wymondham (1 mile)
Nearest Bus Station: Wymondham or East Dereham – each ½ mile away
Car Parking: Available at Dereham Station
Coach Parking: Available at Dereham Station
Souvenir Shop(s): Yes – at Dereham Station
Food & Drinks: Yes – at Dereham Station

SPECIAL INFORMATION

The Mid-Norfolk Railway aims to preserve the former Great Eastern Railway from Wymondham to County School. The section from Wymondham to Dereham was opened to passenger and freight traffic in May 1999 and clearance work is now complete on the East Dereham to County School section.

OPERATING INFORMATION

Opening Times: 2010 dates: Every Sunday and Bank Holiday from 14th March to 24th October. Also open on Saturdays from 20th March to 23rd October, Wednesdays from 5th May to 27th October and Thursdays from 29th July to 26th August.
Steam Working: Weekends and Bank Holidays from 10th July to 30th August inclusive with a visiting Steam locomotive.
Prices: Adult Return £7.00 (Diesel)
Child Return £3.50 (Diesel)
Adult Return £10.00 (Steam days)
Child Return £5.00 (Steam days)

Detailed Directions by Car:
From All Parts: From the A47 bypass, turn into Dereham and follow the signs for the Town Centre. Turn right at the BP Garage – look out for the brown tourist signs – you will see the Station on your right.

MID-SUFFOLK LIGHT RAILWAY MUSEUM

Address: Brockford Station,
Wetheringsett, Suffolk   IP14 5PW
Telephone Nº: (01449) 766899
Year Formed: 1990
Location of Line: Wetheringsett, Suffolk
Length of Line: ¼ mile

Nº of Steam Locos: 2 (1 operational)
Nº of Other Locos: 1
Nº of Members: 400
Annual Membership Fee: £12.00
Approx Nº of Visitors P.A.: 2,000
Gauge: Standard
Web site: www.mslr.org.uk

GENERAL INFORMATION

Nearest Mainline Station: Stowmarket
Nearest Bus Station: Ipswich
Car Parking: Available on site
Coach Parking: Available on site
Souvenir Shop(s): Yes
Food & Drinks: Yes

SPECIAL INFORMATION

The Mid-Suffolk Light Railway served the heart of
the county for 50 years, despite being bankrupt
before the first train ran. In a beautiful rural setting,
the Museum seeks to preserve the memory of a
unique branch line.

OPERATING INFORMATION

Opening Times: Sundays and Bank Holiday
Mondays from Easter to the end of September and
also on Wednesdays in August. Open from 11.00am
to 5.00pm. Special events open at different times.
Steam Working: 2010 dates: 4th & 5th April;
2nd, 3rd, 30th & 31st May; 6th June; 4th July;
1st, 8th, 12th, 15th, 22nd, 29th & 30th August;
26th September. Possibly other dates – please
contact the railway or check the web site for details.
Prices: Adult £5.00   Child £2.50
          Family Ticket £12.50
Tickets allow unlimited travel on the day of issue
and act as season tickets for the calendar year
(subject to conditions).

Detailed Directions by Car:
The Museum is situated 14 miles north of Ipswich and 28 miles south of Norwich, just off the A140. Look for
Mendlesham TV mast and then follow the brown tourist signs from the A140.

NENE VALLEY RAILWAY

Address: Wansford Station, Stibbington, Peterborough   PE8 6LR
Telephone N°: (01780) 784444 enquiries; (01780) 784404 talking timetable
Year Formed: 1977
Location: Off A1 to west of Peterborough
Length of Line: 7½ miles

N° of Steam Locos: 17
N° of Other Locos: 11
N° of Members: 1,300
Annual Membership Fee: Adult £14.50; Child £8.50; Joint £22.00; OAP £8.50
Approx N° of Visitors P.A.: 65,000
Gauge: Standard
Web site: www.nvr.org.uk

GENERAL INFORMATION

Nearest Mainline Station: Peterborough (¾ mile)
Nearest Bus Station: Peterborough (Queensgate – ¾ mile)
Car Parking: Free parking at Wansford & Orton Mere
Coach Parking: Free coach parking at Wansford
Souvenir Shop(s): Yes
Food & Drinks: Yes

SPECIAL INFORMATION

The railway is truly international in flavour with British and Continental locomotives and rolling stock.

OPERATING INFORMATION

Opening Times: 2010 dates: Most weekends from March to 1st November. Also open mid-week on various dates from May to the end of August and also at various other times. Santa Specials run in December. Please contact the Railway for further details. Open 9.00am to 4.30pm.
Steam Working: Most services are steam hauled apart from on diesel days and times of high fire risk.
Prices: Adult £12.00 (Special events £14.00)
Child £6.00 (age 3-15) (Special events £7.00)
Family £30.00 (2 adult + 3 child) (Special £35.00)
Senior Citizens/Disabled £9.00 (Special £10.50)

Detailed Directions by Car:
The railway is situated off the southbound carriageway of the A1 between the A47 and A605 junctions – west of Peterborough and south of Stamford.

NORTH INGS FARM MUSEUM

Address: Fen Road, Dorrington,
Lincoln   LN4 3QB
Telephone Nº: (01526) 833100
Year Formed: 1971
Location of Line: Dorrington
Length of Line: A third of a mile

Nº of Steam Locos: 1
Nº of Other Locos: 8
Approx Nº of Visitors P.A.: –
Gauge: 2 feet
Website: www.northingsfarmmuseum.co.uk

GENERAL INFORMATION

Nearest Mainline Station: Ruskington (3 miles)
Nearest Bus Station: Dorrington (1 mile)
Car Parking: Free parking available on site
Coach Parking: Free parking available on site
Souvenir Shop(s): None
Food & Drinks: None

SPECIAL INFORMATION

The railway forms part of an agricultural machinery
and tractor museum, originally built to serve the
farm.

OPERATING INFORMATION

Opening Times: The first Sunday of the month
from April through to October inclusive. Open from
10.00am to 5.00pm
Steam Working: Subject to availability. Please
contact the Farm Museum for further information.
Prices: Adult £3.00
  Child £1.50

Detailed Directions by Car:
From All Parts: North Ings Farm Museum is situated just off the B1188 between Lincoln and Sleaford. Turn into
Dorrington Village at the Musician's Arms public house, pass through the village and under the railway bridge.
The Museum entrance is on the right after 600 yards and the Museum is then ½ mile down the farm road.

NORTH NORFOLK MODEL ENGINEERING CLUB

Address: c/o Holt Station, Cromer Road, Holt, Norfolk
Telephone Nº: None
Year Formed: 1992
Location of Line: Holt Station Yard
Length of Line: 1,000 feet

Nº of Steam Locos: 10
Nº of Other Locos: 8
Nº of Members: Approximately 45
Approx Nº of Visitors P.A.: 2,000
Gauge: 3½ inches and 5 inches

GENERAL INFORMATION

Nearest Mainline Station: Sheringham (6 miles)
Nearest Bus Stop: 300 yards
Car Parking: Available on site
Coach Parking: None
Souvenir Shop(s): In Holt Station
Food & Drinks: Snacks from Holt Station shop

SPECIAL INFORMATION

North Norfolk Model Engineering Club operates a miniature railway in the yard of Holt Station on the North Norfolk Railway. For details about the NNR please phone (01263) 820800 or check their web site: www.nnr.co.uk

OPERATING INFORMATION

Opening Times: Most Sunday afternoons from April to October inclusive. However, this depends on the availability of drivers, locos and the weather! Also open during most North Norfolk Railway special events.
Steam Working: Most Sundays during the Summer and also during NNR special events.
Prices: No charge but donations are appreciated.

Detailed Directions by Car:
The miniature railway is situated in the yard of Holt Station which is by the side of the A148 Cromer to Fakenham road between the villages of Holt and High Kelling.

NORTH NORFOLK RAILWAY

Address: Sheringham Station, Sheringham, Norfolk NR26 8RA	**N° of Steam Locos**: 5 (+ visiting locos)
Telephone N°: (01263) 820800	**N° of Other Locos**: 4
Year Formed: 1975	**N° of Members**: 1,800 (M&GNRS)
Location of Line: Sheringham to Holt via Weybourne	**Annual Membership Fee**: £18.00
Length of Line: 5½ miles	(Midland & Great Northern Railway Society)
	Approx N° of Visitors P.A.: 130,000
	Gauge: Standard
	Web site: www.nnrailway.co.uk

GENERAL INFORMATION

Nearest Mainline Station: Sheringham (200 yards)
Nearest Bus Station: Outside the Station
Car Parking: Adjacent to Sheringham and Holt
Coach Parking: Adjacent to Sheringham and Holt
Souvenir Shop(s): At Sheringham Station
Food & Drinks: Yes – main catering facilities at Sheringham Station. Light refreshments elsewhere.

SPECIAL INFORMATION

From 11th March 2010, Sheringham level crossing reconnects the North Norfolk Railway with the national network for an occasional use basis, rejoining two former sections of the Midland & Great Northern Joint Railway.

OPERATING INFORMATION

Opening Times: 2010 dates: Daily from 1st April to the 31st October plus weekends in March and Santa Specials in December. Special Events: Vintage Transport Day on 4th July; Beer Festival 16th to 18th July; Grand Steam Gala 3rd to 5th September.
Steam Working: 9.45am to 4.30pm (high season)
Prices: Adult £10.50
  Child £7.00 (Under 5's free of charge)
  Family £35.00 (2 adults + 2 children)
  Senior Citizens £9.50
The prices shown above are for all-day Rover tickets.

Detailed Directions by Car:
Sheringham Station is situated just off the A149. Holt Station is located at High Kelling, just off the A148.

NORTH SCARLE MINIATURE RAILWAY

Address: North Scarle Playing Field, Swinderby Road, North Scarle, Lincolnshire LN6 9ER (for Satnav)
Telephone Nº: (01522) 681424
Year Formed: 1933
Location of Line: North Scarle, between Newark and Lincoln
Length of Line: A third of a mile

Nº of Steam Locos: 7
Nº of Other Locos: 5
Nº of Members: 60
Annual Membership Fee: £24.00
Approx Nº of Visitors P.A.: 3,000
Gauges: 7¼ inches and 5 inches
Web site: www.lincolnmes.co.uk

GENERAL INFORMATION

Nearest Mainline Station: Newark Northgate (5 miles)
Nearest Bus Station: Newark (5 miles)
Car Parking: 300 spaces available on site
Coach Parking: None available
Souvenir Shop(s): None
Food & Drinks: Available on special days only

SPECIAL INFORMATION

The Railway is owned and operated by the Lincoln and District Model Engineering Society which was founded in 1933.

OPERATING INFORMATION

Opening Times: Car Boot Sale Sundays only! Dates for 2010: 28th March; 11th & 25th April; 9th & 23rd May; 6th & 20th June; 4th & 18th July; 1st, 15th & 29th August; 12th & 26th September plus a Special Open Weekend with miniature steam rally including traction engines on 18th & 29th September; October TBA.
Steam Working: Every running day.
Prices: Adult Return 50p
Child Return 50p

Detailed Directions by Car:
North Scarle is situated off the A46 between Lincoln and Newark (about 5 miles from Newark). Alternatively, take the A1133 from Gainsborough and follow the North Scarle signs when around 6 miles from Newark.

NORTHAMPTON SOCIETY OF MODEL ENGINEERS

Correspondence: Hon. Secretary,
Oakwood, 129a High Street, Riseley,
Bedford   MK44 1DJ
Telephone Nº: (01234) 708501
Year Formed: 1933
Location of Line: Lower Delapre Park,
London Road, Northampton

Length of Line: 1,010 feet (raised track)
and 1,700 feet (ground level track)
Nº of Steam Locos: Up to 5 running
Nº of Other Locos: 1 or 2 run occasionally
Nº of Members: 80
Approx Nº of Visitors P.A.: 2,500
Gauge: 3½ inches, 5 inches & 7¼ inches
Web site: www.nsme.co.uk

GENERAL INFORMATION

Nearest Mainline Station: Northampton (2 miles)
Nearest Bus Station: Northampton (2 miles)
Car Parking: Available on site
Coach Parking: On London Road
Food & Drinks: Light refreshments are available

SPECIAL INFORMATION

The Northampton Society of Model Engineers is a
long established society with excellent facilities for
model engineers. The society has over 80 members
with wide ranging interests, several of whom have
won major awards at National exhibitions.

OPERATING INFORMATION

Opening Times: May Day Bank Holiday Monday
then the first Sunday of the month thereafter up to
and including October. Trains run from 2.00pm to
5.00pm.
Steam Working: Every operating day.
Prices: 50p per ride.

Detailed Directions by Car:
From the M1: Exit at Junction 15 and take the A508 to Northampton. Take the 2nd turn off onto the A45 (for the
Town Centre) and then the 2nd exit at the roundabout. After ½ mile turn right just before the pelican crossing
and immediately turn left through the steel gate onto the access track for the railway; From the East: Follow the
A45 and take the turn off signposted for Daventry and the Town Centre. Take the 4th exit at the roundabout onto
the A508, then as above; From the Town Centre: Take the A508 South (Bridge Street). Cross the river and go
straight on at the traffic lights. Pass a petrol station on the left and immediately after the pelican crossing turn left
then immediately left again for the railway.

NORTHAMPTON & LAMPORT RAILWAY

Address: Pitsford & Bramford Station, Pitsford Road, Chapel Brampton, Northampton NN6 8BA **Telephone Nº**: (01604) 820327 (infoline) **Year Formed**: 1983 (became operational in November 1995) **Length of Line**: 1¼ miles at present	**Nº of Steam Locos**: 6 **Nº of Other Locos**: 10 **Nº of Members**: 600 **Annual Membership Fee**: £12.00 **Approx Nº of Visitors P.A.**: 20,000 **Gauge**: Standard **Web site**: www.nlr.org.uk

GENERAL INFORMATION

Nearest Mainline Station: Northampton (5 miles)
Nearest Bus Station: Northampton (5 miles)
Car Parking: Free parking at site
Coach Parking: Free parking at site
Souvenir Shop(s): Yes
Food & Drinks: Yes

SPECIAL INFORMATION

A developing railway – this became operational again on 18th November 1995.

OPERATING INFORMATION

Opening Times: Sundays and Bank holidays in April, May and October. Santa Specials in December. Also on various other detes throughout the year. Open 10.30am to 5.00pm though the last train runs at 3.45pm. Please contact the railway for a more detailed timetable.
Steam Working: Bank Holiday weekends, Santa Specials in December and various other dates. Please contact the railway for further information.
Prices: Adult £4.50
    Child £3.50
    Family £14.50 (2 adults + 2 children)
    Senior Citizen £3.50
Fares may vary on Special Event days.

Detailed Directions by Car:
The station is situated along the Pitsford road at Chapel Brampton, approximately 5 miles north of Northampton. Heading north out of town, it is signposted to the right on the A5199 (A50) Welford Road at Chapel Brampton crossroads or on the left on the A508 Market Harborough road at the Pitsford turn.

NORTHANTS. IRONSTONE RAILWAY TRUST

Address: Hunsbury Hill Museum, Hunsbury Hill Country Park, West Hunsbury, Northampton   NN4 9UW
Telephone Nº: (01604) 702031
Year Formed: 1974
Location of Line: Hunsbury Hill Country Park, Northampton
Length of Line: Two-thirds of a mile

Nº of Steam Locos: 3
Nº of Other Locos: 4
Nº of Members: Approximately 60
Annual Membership Fee: £10.00 Adult
Approx Nº of Visitors P.A.: Not known
Gauge: Standard
Web site: www.nirt.co.uk

GENERAL INFORMATION

Nearest Mainline Station: Northampton (2½ miles)
Nearest Bus Station: Northampton (3 miles)
Car Parking: Large free car park at the site
Coach Parking: Available at the site on request
Souvenir Shop(s): Yes
Food & Drinks: Yes

SPECIAL INFORMATION

The Railway has recently re-opened after a major rebuild and now operates along two-thirds of a mile of track. The Museum is dedicated to the Ironstone industry of Northamptonshire.

OPERATING INFORMATION

Opening Times: The museum is open during Easter weekend then on the first Sunday of the month from May to September and also on Bank Holidays throughout the year. Trains run at these times also. There may also be a number of special events throughout the year (including Santa Specials) – please contact the railway for further details.
Steam Working: An hourly service runs between 11.00am and 5.00pm.
Prices: Adult £3.00   Child £2.00
                   Concessions £1.50
Admission to the museum and site is free of charge but donations are always welcome.

Detailed Directions by Car:
Exit the M1 at Junction 15A, and follow the road for approximately ½ mile. Turn left onto the A43 and after approximately 1 mile take the 3rd exit at the roundabout onto Danes Camp Way (A45). After ½ mile take the 4th exit at the roundabout onto Hunsbury Hill Road. Continue over two mini-roundabouts past the Rose & Claret Public House. The entrance to Hunsbury Hill Country Park for the railway is on the left.

Norwich & District s.m.e.

Correspondence Address: 'Timberlee', Bungay Road, Scole, Diss IP21 4DX
Telephone Nº: (01379) 740578
Year Formed: 1933
Location of Line: Eaton Park, Norwich
Nº of Steam Locos: 5
Nº of Other Locos: 2

Length of Line: Two tracks – one of 800 metres (7¼ and 5 inch gauges) and one of 955 feet (5 and 3½ inch gauges)
Nº of Members: Approximately 120
Approx Nº of Visitors P.A.: 8,000
Gauge: 3½ inches, 5 inches & 7¼ inches

GENERAL INFORMATION

Nearest Mainline Station: Norwich (3 miles)
Nearest Bus Station: Norwich (2 miles)
Car Parking: Available in Eaton Park
Coach Parking: None
Food & Drinks: Available in Eaton Park

SPECIAL INFORMATION

Norwich & District Society of Model Engineers was formed in 1933 and operates two tracks in Eaton Park, one raised and the other ground level.

OPERATING INFORMATION

Opening Times: Sundays during the busy season. Trains run from 2.00pm to 5.00pm. Please contact the railway for further details.
Steam Working: Every operating day.
Prices: £1.00 per ride on the long track
(only open on alternating Sundays)
50p per ride on the short track

Detailed Directions by Car:
Take the A11 or A140 into Norwich and upon reaching the ring road, turn left. At the second set of traffic lights turn left into South Park Avenue and the entrance to Eaton Park is on the right hand side.
Alternative route: Take the A47 into Norwich and turn right at the ring road. At the 3rd set of traffic lights turn right into South Park Avenue.

NOTTINGHAM S.M.E.E

Address: Nottingham Transport Heritage Centre, Mere Way, Ruddington, Nottingham   NG11 6NX
Telephone Nº: None
Year Formed: 1929
Location of Line: Nottingham Transport Heritate Centre, Ruddington
Length of Line: ½ mile

Nº of Steam Locos: Several
Nº of Other Locos: Several
Nº of Members: Approximately 180
Approx Nº of Visitors P.A.: 12,000
Gauge: 3½ inches, 5 inches & 7¼ inches
Web site: www.nsmee.com

GENERAL INFORMATION

Nearest Mainline Station: Nottingham (5 miles)
Nearest Bus Station: Bus service from Nottingham to the Centre
Car Parking: Free parking at site
Coach Parking: Free parking at site
Souvenir Shop(s): Yes
Food & Drinks: Yes

SPECIAL INFORMATION

The Nottingham Society of Model & Experimental Engineers relocated to the Nottingham Heritage Centre in 1992 and have since spent thousands of man-hours constructing multiple tracks for different train gauges.

OPERATING INFORMATION

Opening Times: Sundays from Easter until the end of September. Open 10.00am to 4.30pm.
Steam Working: Most services are steam-hauled.
Prices: Adults 50p per ride
          Children 30p per ride

Detailed Directions by Car:
From All Parts: The centre is situated off the A60 Nottingham to Loughborough Road and is signposted just south of the traffic lights at Ruddington.

PEAK RAIL PLC

Address: Matlock Station, Matlock, Derbyshire   DE4 3NA
Telephone Nº: (01629) 580381
Fax Nº: (01629) 760645
Year Formed: 1975
Location of Line: Matlock Riverside to Rowsley South

Length of Line: Approximately 4 miles
Nº of Steam Locos: 5   **Other Locos:** 20+
Nº of Members: 1,700
Annual Adult Membership Fee: £16.00
Approx Nº of Visitors P.A.: 60,000
Gauge: Standard
Web site: www.peakrail.co.uk

GENERAL INFO

Nearest Mainline Station: Matlock (500 yards)
Nearest Bus Station: Matlock
Car Parking: Paid car parking at Matlock Station. 200 free parking spaces available at Rowsley South Station and 20 free spaces at Darley Dale Station
Coach Parking: Free parking at Rowsley South
Souvenir Shop(s): Yes
Food & Drinks: Yes

SPECIAL INFO

The Palatine Restaurant Car is available whilst travelling on the train and caters for Sunday Lunches, Teas and Party Bookings. Coach parties are welcomed when the railway is operating.

OPERATING INFO

Opening Times: Sundays in January, February and November. Weekends during the rest of the year. Also Wednesdays in May, June and July, Tuesdays and Wednesdays in August and the first two weeks of September.
Steam Working: All services throughout the year.
Prices: Adult Return £6.50
Children – Under-3's Free
Children – Ages 3-5 £1.50
Children – Ages 6-15 £3.50
Senior Citizen Return £5.10
Family Ticket £19.50
(2 adults + 3 children)

Detailed Directions by Car:
Exit the M1 at Junctions 28, 29 or 30 and follow signs towards Matlock. From North and South take A6 direct to Matlock. From Stoke-on-Trent, take the A52 to Ashbourne, then the A5035 to Matlock. Upon reaching Matlock follow the brown tourist signs.

PETTITTS ANIMAL ADVENTURE PARK RAILWAY

Address: Church Road, Reedham, NR13 3UA	**N⁰ of Steam Locos**: None
Telephone N⁰: (01493) 700094	**N⁰ of Other Locos**: 1
Year Formed: 1989	**N⁰ of Members**: –
Location of Line: 10 miles to the west of Great Yarmouth	**Approx N⁰ of Visitors P.A.**: 100,000 (to the Park itself)
Length of Line: 500 yards	**Gauge**: 10¼ inches
	Web site: www.pettittsadventurepark.co.uk

GENERAL INFORMATION

Nearest Mainline Station: Reedham (½ mile)
Nearest Bus Station: Great Yarmouth (10 miles)
Car Parking: Available on site
Coach Parking: Available
Souvenir Shop(s): Yes
Food & Drinks: Available

SPECIAL INFORMATION

The railway runs within an adventure park which has extensive facilities for a good family day out.

OPERATING INFORMATION

Opening Times: 2010 dates: Daily from 27th March to 31st October, 10.00am to 5.00pm.
Steam Working: None at present
Prices: Adults £9.95
Children £9.95 (Free for the Under-3s)
Concessions £7.95
Family Ticket £39.00
Note: The prices shown above are for admission to the Park and include rides on the railway.

Detailed Directions by Car:
From All Parts: Take the A47 Norwich to Great Yarmouth road to Acle and follow the brown tourist signs southwards to Reedham for the Park.

QUEEN'S PARK MINIATURE RAILWAY

Address: Queen's Park, Boythorpe Road, Chesterfield   S40 2BF
Telephone Nº: (01246) 345777
Year Formed: 1976
Location of Line:
Length of Line: 550 yards

Nº of Steam Locos: None
Nº of Other Locos: 1
Approx Nº of Visitors P.A.: 350,000 (to the Park itself)
Gauge: 10¼ inches
Web site: www.chesterfield.gov.uk/default.aspx?CATID=761&CID=4097

GENERAL INFORMATION

Nearest Mainline Station: Chesterfield (1 mile)
Nearest Bus Station: Chesterfield (¼ mile)
Car Parking: Available on site
Coach Parking: Available
Souvenir Shop(s): None
Food & Drinks: Available

SPECIAL INFORMATION

The railway runs through a 22-acre Green Flag listed park which was opened in 1887 to commemorate Queen Victoria's Golden Jubilee.

OPERATING INFORMATION

Opening Times: Daily from Easter to the end of September, from 11.00am to 5.00pm.
Steam Working: None
Prices: Adults £1.50
　　　　　Children £1.50 (Free for Under-3s)

Detailed Directions by Car:
From All Parts: Exit the M1 at Junction 29 and take the A617 into Chesterfield. Turn left at the 2nd roundabout following signs for Matlock/Buxton and then left onto the A632 at the next roundabout signposted for Matlock. The Park is on the right after approximately 200 yards.

RAINSBROOK VALLEY RAILWAY

Address: Rugby Model Engineering Society, Onley Lane, Rugby CV22 5QD
Telephone Nº: (01788) 330238
Year Formed: 1949
Location of Line: Onley Lane, Rugby
Length of Line: 1,100 yards (7¼ inch) and 1,100 feet (3½ & 5 inch gauges)

Nº of Steam Locos: 10
Nº of Other Locos: 4+
Nº of Members: 80
Annual Membership Fee: £45.00
Approx Nº of Visitors P.A.: 5,500
Gauges: 3½ inches, 5 inches & 7¼ inches
Web site: www.rugbymes.co.uk

GENERAL INFORMATION

Nearest Mainline Station: Rugby (2½ miles)
Nearest Bus Station: Rugby (2½ miles)
Car Parking: Available on site
Coach Parking: None
Souvenir Shop(s): None
Food & Drinks: Light refreshments only

SPECIAL INFORMATION

The Rainsbrook Valley Railway is operated by members of the Rugby Model Engineering Society.

OPERATING INFORMATION

Opening Times: 2010 dates: 18th April, 16th May, 20th June, 18th July, 15th August, 26th September and 17th October.
Steam Working: Trains run from 2.00pm to 5.00pm
Prices: £1.00 per ride (Under-3s travel free)

Detailed Directions by Car:
From the M1: Exit at Junction 18 and follow the A428 westwards towards Rugby. After 3 miles turn left on to the B4429 towards Dunchurch. After 1 mile turn left at the crossroads into Onley Lane and the Railway is on the right hand side after 300 yards; From Dunchurch: Follow the A426 Northwards then turn onto the B4429 at the roundabout travelling Eastwards. After 1 mile turn right at the crossroads into Onley Lane for the Railway; From Rugby: In Rugby, follow signs for the Hospital in Barby Road then continue South for 1 mile. At the crossroads go straight on over the B4429 into Onley Lane for the Railway.

RUDYARD LAKE STEAM RAILWAY

Address: Rudyard Station, Rudyard, Near Leek, Staffordshire ST13 8PF	**N⁰ of Steam Locos:** 5

Address: Rudyard Station, Rudyard,
Near Leek, Staffordshire   ST13 8PF
Telephone N⁰: (01538) 306704
Year Formed: 1985
Location: Rudyard to Hunthouse Wood
Length of Line: 1½ miles

N⁰ of Steam Locos: 5
N⁰ of Other Locos: 3
N⁰ of Members: –
Approx N⁰ of Visitors P.A.: 40,000
Gauge: 10¼ inches and 7¼ inches
Web site: www.rudyardlakerailway.co.uk

GENERAL INFORMATION

Nearest Mainline Station: Stoke-on-Trent (10 miles)
Nearest Bus Station: Leek
Car Parking: Free parking at Rudyard Station
Coach Parking: Free parking at Rudyard Station
Souvenir Shop(s): Yes
Food & Drinks: Yes – Cafe open at weekends

SPECIAL INFORMATION

The Railway runs along the side of the historic
Rudyard Lake that gave author Rudyard Kipling his
name. A Steamboat also plies the lake at times.
"Drive a Steam Train" courses can be booked or
bought as a gift with vouchers valid for 9 months.
A short 7¼ inch gauge railway operates on special
event days.

OPERATING INFORMATION

Opening Times: 2010 dates: Every Sunday and
Bank Holiday from January to the end of November.
Also open on every Saturday from 3rd April to 30th
October and Monday to Friday from 29th March to
11th April, 26th May to 4th June, 21st July to 5th
September and 25th to 29th October. Santa Specials
run on 18th & 19th December and there is a Steam
Gala on 25th & 26th September.
Steam Working: All trains are normally steam
hauled. Trains run from 11.00am and the last train
runs around 4.00pm.
Prices: Adult Return £3.50
         Child Return £2.50
A variety of other fares and Day Rover tickets are
also available.

Detailed Directions by Car:
From All Parts: Head for Leek then follow the A523 North towards Macclesfield for 1 mile. Follow the brown
tourist signs to the B5331 signposted for Rudyard for ½ mile. Pass under the Railway bridge and turn immediately
left and go up the ramp to the Station car park.

RUSHDEN TRANSPORT MUSEUM

Address: Rushden Station, Station Approach, Rushden, NN10 0AW
Telephone Nº: (01933) 318988
Year Formed: 1985
Location of Line: Rushden, Northants.
Length of Line: ¼ mile

Nº of Steam Locos: 3
Nº of Other Locos: 3
Nº of Members: Approximately 600
Annual Membership Fee: –
Approx Nº of Visitors P.A.: 5,000
Gauge: Standard
Web site: www.rhts.co.uk

GENERAL INFORMATION

Nearest Mainline Station: Wellingborough (5 miles)
Nearest Bus Station: Northampton (14 miles)
Car Parking: Available on site. On operating days a nearby public car park must be used.
Coach Parking: None
Souvenir Shop(s): Yes
Food & Drinks: Available on operating weekends

SPECIAL INFORMATION

The Rushden Transport Museum is situated in the old Midland Railway Station of 1894 which once formed part of the Wellingborough to Higham Ferrers branch line. Taken over by the Rushden Historical Transport Society in 1984 the station also provides the society with a social club.

OPERATING INFORMATION

Opening Times: Sundays from Easter until the end of October, open from 10.00am to 4.00pm. Trains operate on one weekend a month. Please contact the Museum or check the web site for further details.
Steam Working: Please contact the Museum for further details.
Prices: Adults £3.00
Children £1.50
Concessions £1.50
Note: Higher prices may be charged during special event days.

Detailed Directions by Car:
From All Parts: Take the A6 to the Rushden Bypass (to the south of the A45) and turn into John Clark Way by the large grey warehouses. The Station is located on the right-hand side of the road after approximately 400 yards.

RUTLAND RAILWAY MUSEUM

Address: Cottesmore Iron Ore Mines Siding, Ashwell Road, Cottesmore, Oakham, Rutland LE15 7BX	**Nº of Steam Locos**: 13
Telephone Nº: (01572) 813203	**Nº of Other Locos**: 13
Year Formed: 1979	**Nº of Members**: 275
Location of Line: Between the villages of Cottesmore and Ashwell	**Annual Membership Fee**: £10.00
	Approx Nº of Visitors P.A.: 8,000
	Gauge: Standard
Length of Line: ¾ mile	**Web site**: www.rutlandrailwaymuseum.org.uk

GENERAL INFORMATION

Nearest Mainline Station: Oakham (4 miles)
Nearest Bus Station: Cottesmore/Ashwell (1½ miles)
Car Parking: Available at the site
Coach Parking: Limited space available
Souvenir Shop(s): On open days
Food & Drinks: On open days

SPECIAL INFORMATION

This Industrial Railway Heritage centre is located at the end of the former Ashwell-Cottesmore mineral branch and is based at the former exchange sidings.

OPERATING INFORMATION

Opening Times: Static viewing on Sundays from 11.00am to 4.00pm plus Tuesday and Thursday afternoons throughout the year.
Steam Working: 2010 dates: Santa Specials run on on 19th & 20th December. Please contact the railway for further details and dates for other events. Pre-booked Driver experience days are available.
Prices: Adult £4.00
            Child £2.00 (no charge for under 5's)
Prices shown are for admission to the site on steam operating days. Train rides are an additional fee. Special prices apply to Santa Specials in December.

Detailed Directions by Car:
From All Parts: The Museum is situated 4 miles north of Oakham between Ashwell and Cottesmore. Follow the brown tourist signs from the B668 Oakham to A1 road or the signs from the A606 Stamford to Oakham Road.

SAFFRON WALDEN & DISTRICT S.M.E.

Correspondence: The Secretary, 'Baltana', London Road, Barkway, Royston SG8 8EY	**Length of Line**: 1,500 feet
	Nº of Steam Locos: 14
	Nº of Other Locos: 8
Telephone Nº: (01763) 848228	**Nº of Members**: 50
Year Formed: 1980	**Approx Nº of Visitors P.A.**: 2,500
Location of Line: Audley End Miniature Railway	**Gauge**: 3½ inches, 5 inches & 7¼ inches
	Web site: www.swdsme.org.uk

GENERAL INFORMATION

Nearest Mainline Station: Audley End (1 mile)
Nearest Bus Station: Saffron Walden (1 mile)
Car Parking: Available on site
Coach Parking: Available on site
Souvenir Shop(s): Yes
Food & Drinks: Snacks available

SPECIAL INFORMATION

The Saffron Walden & District Society of Model Engineers uses a track at Audley End Steam Railway, Lord Braybrooke's private 10¼ inch railway situated just next to Audley End House, an English Heritage site.

OPERATING INFORMATION

Opening Times: Most Saturdays and Sundays from April to October inclusive. Trains run from 2.00pm to 5.00pm.
Steam Working: Most operating days.
Prices: £1.00 per ride (A Multi-ticket is £3.00)

Detailed Directions by Car:
Exit the M11 at Junction 10 if southbound or Junction 9 if northbound and follow the signs for Audley End House. The railway is situated just across the road from Audley End House.

SCUNTHORPE SOCIETY OF MODEL ENGINEERS

Address: Normanby Hall Country Park,
Normanby   DN15 9HU
Telephone N°: (01724) 720588
Year Formed: 1935 (at a different site)
Location of Line: North Lincolnshire
Length of Line: One third of a mile
N° of Steam Locos: Approximately 14

N° of Other Locos: Approximately 17
N° of Members: Approximately 100
Annual Membership Fee: £10.00
Approx N° of Visitors P.A.: 170,000 (to the Country Park)
Gauges: 3½ inches and 5 inches
Web site: www.scunthorpesme.co.uk

GENERAL INFORMATION

Nearest Mainline Station: Scunthorpe (3 miles)
Nearest Bus Station: Scunthorpe (3 miles)
Car Parking: Available on site
Coach Parking: Available
Souvenir Shop(s): Yes
Food & Drinks: Available

SPECIAL INFORMATION

The Society operates in the historic Normanby Hall
Country Park, the home of the Sheffield family.

OPERATING INFORMATION

Opening Times: Sundays and Bank Holiday
Mondays from Easter to the end of September.
Trains run from 1.00pm to 4.30pm.
Steam Working: Most operating days.
Prices: Adults £5.10 (Admission to the Park)
            Children £2.55 (Admission to the Park)
            Concessions £4.60 (Admission to Park)
Note: Rides are an addition 20p per person.

Detailed Directions by Car:
From All Parts: Normanby Hall is located off the B1430 road to the north of Scunthorpe. Take the A1077 Barton
Road to Crosby roundabout by Astle Motors then follow the brown tourist signs for Normanby Hall.

SEVERN VALLEY RAILWAY

Address: Railway Station, Bewdley, Worcestershire DY12 1BG	**Nº of Steam Locos**: 27
Telephone Nº: (01299) 403816	**Nº of Other Locos**: 12
Year Formed: 1965	**Nº of Members**: 13,000
Location of Line: Kidderminster (Worcs.) to Bridgnorth (Shropshire)	**Annual Membership Fee**: Adult £17.00
	Approx Nº of Passengers P.A.: 248,000
	Gauge: Standard
Length of Line: 16 miles	**Web site**: www.svr.co.uk

GENERAL INFORMATION

Nearest Mainline Station: Kidderminster (adjacent)
Nearest Bus Station: Kidderminster (500 yards)
Car Parking: Large car park at Kidderminster. Spaces also available at other stations.
Coach Parking: At Kidderminster
Souvenir Shop(s): At Kidderminster & Bridgnorth
Food & Drinks: On most trains. Also at Bewdley, Bridgnorth, Kidderminster and The Engine House

SPECIAL INFORMATION

The SVR has numerous special events including an Autumn Steam Gala, 1940's weekend, Classic Car & Bike Day and visits by Santa! 'The Engine House', the railway's visitor and education centre, is a further attraction at Highley.

OPERATING INFORMATION

Opening Times: 2010 dates: Weekends throughout the year. Also daily from 1st May to 3rd October and during local School Holidays.
Steam Working: Train times vary depending on timetable information. Phone for details.
Prices: Adult Day Rover £15.50
Child Day Rover £8.00
Senior Citizen Day Rover £13.50
Family Day Rover £42.00
(2 adults + 4 children)
Note: Entrance to The Engine House is now included in the prices listed above.

Detailed Directions by Car:
For Kidderminster take M5 and exit Junction 3 or Junction 6. Follow the brown tourist signs for the railway; From the South: Take the M40 then M42 to Junction 1 for the A448 from Bromsgrove to Kidderminster.

SHERWOOD FOREST RAILWAY

Address: Sherwood Forest Farm Park, Edwinstowe, Mansfield NG21 9HL	**No of Steam Locos**: 2
Telephone No: (01623) 515339	**No of Other Locos**: 3
Year Formed: 1999	**No of Members**: 13
Location of Line: Between Mansfield Woodhouse and Edwinstowe	**Annual Membership Fee**: –
	Approx No of Visitors P.A.: 17,000
	Gauge: 15 inches
Length of Line: 680 yards	**Web site**: www.sherwoodforestrailway.com

GENERAL INFORMATION

Nearest Mainline Station: Mansfield (7 miles)
Nearest Bus Station: Mansfield (7 miles)
Car Parking: Free parking available on site
Coach Parking: Available on site
Souvenir Shop(s): Yes
Food & Drinks: Available

SPECIAL INFORMATION

The Railway runs through the grounds of a 26 acre Farm Park which contains hundreds of rare breeds of animals, terraced flower gardens, a small petting area and play areas for children.

OPERATING INFORMATION

Opening Times: 2010 dates: Daily from 2nd April until 28th September. The Farm Park is open from 10.30am and trains run until 5.00pm.
Steam Working: Every operating day
Prices: Adults £1.00 (Allows rides for a week)
Chidren £1.00 (Allows rides for a week)
Family £4.00 (Allows rides for a week)
Farm Park Entrance Charges:
Adults £6.50
Concessions £5.50
Children £4.50 (Under 3s admitted free)
Family £20.00

Detailed Directions by Car:
From the A1: Turn off at the Worksop roundabout and head to Ollerton. Follow the A6075 through Edwinstowe and towards Mansfield Woodhouse, then turn left at the double mini-roundabout. The Farm Park is on the right after approximately 200 yards; From Nottingham: Head to Ollerton, then as above; From the M1: Exit at Junction 27 and head into Mansfield. Follow signs to Mansfield Woodhouse and then on towards Edwinstowe. From here, follow the tourist signs for the Farm Park.

SNIBSTON COLLIERY RAILWAY

Address: Ashby Road, Coalville, LE67 3LN	**Nº of Steam Locos**: 4
Telephone Nº: (01530) 278444	**Nº of Other Locos**: 2
Year Formed: 2001	**Nº of Members**: –
Location of Line: Snibston Colliery	**Approx Nº of Visitors P.A.**: 100,000
Length of Line: 1,100 yards	**Gauge**: Standard
	Web site: www.snibston.com

GENERAL INFORMATION

Nearest Mainline Station: Loughborough (10 miles)
Nearest Bus Station: Loughborough (10 miles)
Car Parking: Available on site
Coach Parking: Available on site
Souvenir Shop(s): Yes
Food & Drinks: Available

SPECIAL INFORMATION

The Railway is located on the site of the former Snibston Colliery which also hosts an interactive museum, outside play areas, a Country Park and a nature reserve.

OPERATING INFORMATION

Opening Times: The museum is open daily except for Christmas Day, Boxing Day and a two week break in January. Open from 10.00am to 3.00pm or 4.00pm, depending on the time of the year. Trains operate only on certain dates. Please contact the Museum for further information.

Steam Working: No usual steam operation. Please contact the Museum for details.

Prices: Adults £6.75 (Train rides £1.25 extra)
Children £4.50 (Trains rides 75p extra)
Concessions £4.75 (Train rides £1.25 extra)
Family £20.00 (2+2) or £22.00 (2 + 3)
(Train rides £3.20 extra)

Detailed Directions by Car:
From All Parts: Exit the A42 at the A511 (Coalville) exit and follow the signs for Snibston.

Stapleford Miniature Railway

Address: Stapleford Park, Stapleford, Melton Mowbray, Leicestershire
Telephone N⁰: (01949) 860138
Year Formed: 1957
Location of Line: Stapleford Park
Length of Line: 2 miles
Web site: www.fsmr.org.uk

N⁰ of Steam Locos: 6
N⁰ of Other Locos: 1
N⁰ of Members: 45
Annual Membership Fee: By invitation
Approx N⁰ of Visitors P.A.: Not known
Gauge: $10\frac{1}{4}$ inches

GENERAL INFORMATION

Nearest Mainline Station: Melton Mowbray (4 miles)
Nearest Bus Station: Melton Mowbray (4 miles)
Car Parking: Available on site
Coach Parking: Available on site
Souvenir Shop(s): Yes
Food & Drinks: Available – including a licensed bar

SPECIAL INFORMATION

The railway is only open to the public for two weekends a year as shown. The June event is run in conjunction with a Steam Rally and various traction engines will be on site. The August event concentrates on the railway with other smaller attractions. Weekend camping is available at both events. Please check the web site for details.

OPERATING INFORMATION

Opening Times: 2010 dates: 19th and 20th June, 29th and 30th August.
Steam Working: All trains on the open weekends
Prices: Adult £5.00 (June event)
Child/Senior Citizen £3.00 (June event)
Note: Train rides are an additional small charge. Family Tickets are available for the June event. Entrance to the August event is £3.00 per car.

Detailed Directions by Car:
The railway is located off the B676 Melton Mowbray to Colsterworth road about 4 miles to the East of Melton Mowbray. The Stapleford Park Hotel is well-signposted with brown tourist signs and follow these to turn off the B676. The railway is located on the left hand side just before Stapleford Village and the turn into the hotel.

STEEPLE GRANGE LIGHT RAILWAY

Address: High Peak Trail, Near National Stone Centre, Wirksworth   DE4 4LS
Telephone Nº: (01629) 580917
Year Formed: 1986
Location of Line: Off the High Peak trail near Wirksworth
Length of Line: ½ mile at present

Nº of Steam Locos: 1 (awaiting rebuild)
Nº of Other Locos: 17
Nº of Members: 150
Annual Membership Fee: From £6.00
Approx Nº of Visitors P.A.: 8,000+
Gauge: 18 inches
Web site: www.steeplegrange.co.uk

GENERAL INFORMATION

Nearest Mainline Station: Cromford (2 miles)
Nearest Bus Station: Matlock
Car Parking: Free parking available nearby
Coach Parking: Free parking available nearby
Souvenir Shop(s): Yes
Food & Drinks: Light refreshments available

SPECIAL INFORMATION

The Railway is built on the track bed of the former Standard Gauge Cromford and High Peak Railway branch to Middleton. The railway uses mostly former mining/quarrying rolling stock and has two separate lines operating.

OPERATING INFORMATION

Opening Times: Sundays and Bank Holidays from Easter until the end of October. Also open on Saturdays from July to September and by prior arrangement. Special Events at other times of the year including Santa Specials on dates in December. Please contact the railway for further details.
Trains run from 12.00pm to 5.00pm
Steam Working: None at present
Prices: Adult Return £2.00
                    Child Return £1.00
                    Family Return £5.00
Note: Special fares apply during special events and also for group bookings.

Detailed Directions by Car:
The Railway is situated adjacent to the National Stone Centre just to the north of Wirksworth at the junction of the B5035 and B5036. Free car parking is available at the National Stone Centre and in Old Porter Lane.

STRUMPSHAW STEAM MUSEUM

Address: Low Road, Strumpshaw, Norwich NR13 4HR	**Nº of Steam Locos**: Various steam vehicles
Telephone Nº: (01603) 714535	**Nº of Other Locos**: are on display
Year Formed: 1954	**Approx Nº of Visitors P.A.**: Not known
Location of Line: Near Norwich	**Gauge**: 2 feet
Length of Line: 680 yards	**Web site**: www.strumpshawsteammuseum.co.uk

Regrettably, no suitable photograph of the railway was available at the time of going to press.

GENERAL INFORMATION

Nearest Mainline Station: Buckenham (1½ miles)
Nearest Bus Station: Norwich (10 miles)
Car Parking: Available on site
Coach Parking: Available
Souvenir Shop(s): Yes
Food & Drinks: Available

SPECIAL INFORMATION

The museum houses steam engines and various kinds of mechanical and steam memorabilia.

OPERATING INFORMATION

Opening Times: 2010 dates: Daily during Easter week then Sundays, Wednesdays and Bank Holidays from 11th April to 27th June. Then daily from 28th June to 3rd October. Open from 10.30am to 3.30pm.
Steam Working: The last Sunday of each month plus a Steam Rally on 29th, 30th and 31st May 2010.
Prices: Adults £8.00 (during the Steam Rally)
Ages 13 to 15 £2.00 (during the Steam Rally)
Under-12s are admitted free to the Rally
Please contact the museum for details of pricing information on other dates.
Note: Dogs on leads are welcome at the museum!

Detailed Directions by Car:
From All Parts: The museum is located to the south of the A47 Norwich to Acle road. Leave the A47 at the Brundall Roundabout then turn first left by the petrol station into Blofield Road. Turn right at the traffic lights into Stocks Lane then turn left at the mini-roundabout along Strumpshaw Road. At Strumpshaw follow signs for the museum.

SUMMERFIELDS MINIATURE RAILWAY

Address: Summerfields Farm, Haynes, Bedford MK45 3BH	**N° of Steam Locos**: 8
Telephone N°: (01234) 301867	**N° of Other Locos**: 7
Year Formed: 1948	**N° of Members**: Approximately 180
Location: Off the A600, North of Haynes	**Annual Membership Fee**: £32.00
Length of Line: Approximately ¾ mile	**Approx N° of Visitors P.A.**: 10,000
	Gauge: 7¼ inches
	Web site: www.summerfieldsmr.co.uk

GENERAL INFORMATION

Nearest Mainline Station: Bedford (5½ miles)
Nearest Bus Station: Bedford
Car Parking: Available on site
Coach Parking: Available on site
Souvenir Shop(s): None
Food & Drinks: Available

SPECIAL INFORMATION

Summerfields Miniature Railway is operated by the Bedford Model Engineering Society.

OPERATING INFORMATION

Opening Times: Opening times vary – please phone for details.
Steam Working: On all public running days
Prices: Adult Return £1.50
Child Return £1.50

Detailed Directions by Car:
From All Parts: The Railway is located by the A600 just to the North of Haynes, 5½ miles South of Bedford and 3½ miles North of Shefford.

TELFORD STEAM RAILWAY

Address: The Old Loco Shed, Bridge Road, Horsehay, Telford, Shropshire	**Nº of Steam Locos**: 5
	Nº of Other Locos: 12
Telephone Enquiries: 07876 762790	**Nº of Members**: Approximately 220
Year Formed: 1976	**Annual Membership Fee**: £12.00
Location: Horsehay & Dawley Station	**Approx Nº of Visitors P.A.**: 10,000
Length of Line: ½ mile standard gauge, an eighth of a mile 2 foot narrow gauge	**Web site**: www.telfordsteamrailway.co.uk

GENERAL INFORMATION

Nearest Mainline Station: Wellington or Telford Central
Nearest Bus Station: Dawley (1 mile)
Car Parking: Free parking at the site
Coach Parking: Free parking at the site
Souvenir Shop(s): 'Freight Stop Gift Shop'
Food & Drinks: 'The Furnaces' Tea Room

SPECIAL INFORMATION

Telford Steam Railway has both a Standard Gauge and Narrow Gauge line as well as Miniature and Model Railways. Major line extension works are currently underway.

OPERATING INFORMATION

Opening Times: Every Sunday and Bank Holiday between Easter and the end of September. Santa Specials run in December. Open 11.00am to 4.30pm.
Steam Working: 2 foot gauge on all operating days. Standard gauge on the last Sunday of the month, every Sunday in August and also on Bank Holidays.
Prices: Adult all day tickets £3.00
Child all day tickets £3.00
Family all day tickets £12.00

Detailed Directions by Car:
From All Parts: Exit the M54 at Junction 6, travel south along the A5223 then follow the brown tourist signs for the railway.

TYSELEY LOCOMOTIVE WORKS VISITOR CENTRE

Address: 670 Warwick Road, Tyseley, Birmingham B11 2HL
Telephone Nº: (0121) 708-4960
Year Formed: 1969
Location of Museum: Tyseley
Length of Line: One third of a mile

Nº of Steam Locos: Varies with visiting Locos and restoration contracts
Nº of Members: Approximately 600
Approx Nº of Visitors P.A.: 10,000
Gauge: Standard
Web site: www.vintagetrains.co.uk

GENERAL INFORMATION

Nearest Mainline Station: Tyseley (5 mins. walk)
Nearest Bus Station: Birmingham. Bus Stop at Reddings Lane – 2 minutes walk (Bus route 37 passes the entrance)
Car Parking: 200 spaces at Railway site
Coach Parking: Space at Railway site
Souvenir Shop(s): Yes
Food & Drinks: None

SPECIAL INFORMATION

The Museum runs a large workshop which produces refurbished locomotives, many for operation on Network Rail Lines.

OPERATING INFORMATION

Opening Times: 2010 dates: The Museum open days will be held on 26th and 27th June between the hours of 10.00am and 4.00pm. Further events are planned later in the year. Please contact the museum for further information.
Steam Working: On all open days. The Loco Works also operates mainline excursions from the Museum Station and runs the Shakespeare Express from Birmingham to Stratford-upon-Avon every Sunday from 4th July to 12th September 2010.
Prices: Vary depending on the open day. Shakespeare Express fares start from around £17.50.

Detailed Directions by Car:
From the North: Exit the M6 at Junction 6 and take A41 ring road towards Solihull; From the South: Exit the M42 at Junction 5 and take the A41 towards Birmingham.

WELLS HARBOUR RAILWAY

Address: Wells Harbour Railway, Beach Road, Wells-next-the-Sea NR23 1DR **Telephone Nº**: (07939) 149264 **Year Formed**: 1976 **Location of Line**: Wells-next-the-Sea **Length of Line**: Approximately 1 mile	**Nº of Steam Locos**: 1 **Nº of Other Locos**: 2 **Nº of Members**: None **Approx Nº of Visitors P.A.**: 50,000 **Gauge**: 10¼ inches **Web site**: www.wellsharbourrailway.com

GENERAL INFORMATION

Nearest Mainline Station: King's Lynn (21 miles)
Nearest Bus Station: Norwich (24 miles)
Car Parking: Public car parks near each station
Coach Parking: Available in town
Souvenir Shop(s): No
Food & Drinks: No

SPECIAL INFORMATION

Wells Harbour Railway was the first 10¼" narrow gauge railway to run a scheduled passenger service and is listed in the Guinness Book of Records!

OPERATING INFORMATION

Opening Times: Weekends from Easter until Spring Bank Holiday then daily through to the middle of September. Then weekends until the end of October. The first train departs at 10.30am.
Steam Working: None
Prices: Adult Single £1.20
Child Single £1.00

Detailed Directions by Car:
Wells-next-the-Sea is located on the North Norfolk cost between Hunstanton and Cromer. The railway is situated on Beach Road next to the harbour. Follow the signs for Pinewoods and Beach.

WELLS & WALSINGHAM LIGHT RAILWAY

Address: The Station, Wells-next-the-Sea NR23 1QB	**Nº of Steam Locos**: 1
Telephone Nº: (01328) 711630	**Nº of Other Locos**: 2
Year Formed: 1982	**Nº of Members**: 50
Location of Line: Wells-next-the-Sea to Walsingham, Norfolk	**Annual Membership Fee**: £11.00
	Approx Nº of Visitors P.A.: 20,000
	Gauge: 10¼ inches
Length of Line: 4 miles	**Website**: www.wellswalsinghamrailway.co.uk

GENERAL INFORMATION

Nearest Mainline Station: King's Lynn (21 miles)
Nearest Bus Station: Norwich (24 miles)
Car Parking: Free parking at site
Coach Parking: Free parking at site
Souvenir Shop(s): Yes
Food & Drinks: Yes

SPECIAL INFORMATION

The Railway is the longest 10¼ inch narrow-gauge steam railway in the world. The course of the railway is famous for wildlife and butterflies in season.

OPERATING INFORMATION

Opening Times: 2010 dates: Daily from 2nd April until the end of October.
Steam Working: Trains run from 10.15am on operating days.
Prices: Adult Return £8.00
Child Return £6.50

Detailed Directions by Car:
Wells-next-the-Sea is situated on the North Norfolk Coast midway between Hunstanton and Cromer. The Main Station is situated on the main A149 Stiffkey Road. Follow the brown tourist signs for the Railway.

WESTON PARK RAILWAY

Address: Weston Park, Weston-under-Lizard, Shifnal, Shropshire   TF11 8LE
Telephone Nº: (05601) 132334 (Railway) or (01952) 852100 (Weston Park)
Year Formed: 1980
Location of Line: Weston Park

Length of Line: Approximately 1¼ miles
Nº of Steam Locos: Variable
Nº of Other Locos: Variable
Approx Nº of Visitors P.A.: 19,500
Gauge: 7¼ inches
Web site: www.weston-park.com

GENERAL INFORMATION

Nearest Mainline Station: Shifnal (6 miles)
Nearest Bus Station: –
Car Parking: Available on site
Coach Parking: Available on site
Souvenir Shop(s): –
Food & Drinks: Available

SPECIAL INFORMATION

The railway operates in the grounds of Weston Park, a stately home with a large park and gardens designed by 'Capability' Brown. Weston Park also has a number of other attractions for all the family.

OPERATING INFORMATION

Opening Times: 2010 dates: Daily from 29th May to 5th September. Please contact Weston Park for further details about weekend opening.
Steam Working: Please contact the railway for further details: info@westonrail.co.uk
Prices: Adults £2.00
                Children £1.50
Note: Prices shown above are for train fares only. An admission charge is made for entry into the park, gardens and stately home. This admission fee is required for use of the railway. Please contact Weston Park for admission price information.

Detailed Directions by Car:
From All Parts: Weston Park is situated by the side of the A5 in Weston-under-Lizard, Shropshire, just 3 miles from the M54 (exit at Junction 3 and take the A41 northwards) and 8 miles West of the M6 (exit at Junction 12).

WHITWELL & REEPHAM RAILWAY

Address: Whitwell Road, Reepham,
Norfolk   NR10 4GA
Telephone Nº: (01603) 871694
Year Formed: 2009
Location of Line: Norfolk
Length of Line: Almost ½ mile

Nº of Steam Locos: 1
Nº of Other Locos: 1
Nº of Members: Approximately 400
Annual Membership Fee: £15.00
Approx Nº of Visitors P.A.: 6,000
Gauge: Standard
Web site: www.whitwellstation.com

GENERAL INFORMATION

Nearest Mainline Station: Norwich (15 miles)
Nearest Bus Station: Norwich (15 miles)
Car Parking: Available on site
Coach Parking: Available
Souvenir Shop(s): Yes
Food & Drinks: Available

SPECIAL INFORMATION

Whitwell & Reepham Station re-opened on the 28th
February 2009 nearly 50 years after it was closed to
passengers on 2nd March 1959. The intention is to
restore the Station to its former glory, re-laying of
track and sidings, acquiring rolling stock and setting
up a museum relating to the Station and The
Midland & Great Northern Railway.

OPERATING INFORMATION

Opening Times: Weekends throughout the year
from 10.00am until dusk.
Steam Working: Usually the first Sunday each
month and also on Bank Holidays. Please contact
the Museum for further details.
Prices: Adults £2.00
  Children £1.00
  Family £5.00
Note: Prices shown above are for train rides –
admission to the museum is free of charge.

Detailed Directions by Car:
From All Parts: Take the A1067 Norwich to Fakenham Road to Bawdeswell then follow the B1145 to Reepham.
The railway is located about 1 mile to the South-west of Reepham and is well-signposted.

WICKSTEED PARK RAILWAY

Address: Wicksteed Park, Kettering, NN15 6NJ
Telephone Nº: 08700 621194
Year Formed: 1931
Location of Line: Wicksteed Park
Length of Line: 1¼ miles

Nº of Steam Locos: None
Nº of Other Locos: 3
Approx Nº of Visitors P.A.: 180,000
Gauge: 2 feet
Web site: www.wicksteedpark.co.uk

GENERAL INFORMATION

Nearest Mainline Station: Kettering (2 miles)
Nearest Bus Station: Kettering (2 miles)
Car Parking: Available on site (£6.00 entrance fee per car)
Coach Parking: Free parking available on site
Souvenir Shop(s): Yes
Food & Drinks: Available

SPECIAL INFORMATION

The Railway runs through the grounds of a large leisure complex, Wicksteed Park, which also houses many other attractions including a fairground, a rollercoaster and a log chute ride.

OPERATING INFORMATION

Opening Times: 2010 dates: Open at weekends from 27th March to 31st October and daily during the school holidays. Open from 10.30am to 6.00pm in the Summer and until 4.30pm at other times.
Steam Working: Steam Weekend – 11th & 12th July
Prices: As a wide variety of rides are available, sheets of ride tickets can be purchased at a rate of £11.00 for 12 tickets or £20.00 for 30 tickets. Each trip on the railway costs 2 ride tickets. Alternatively wristbands which allow unlimited use of all attractions on the day of purchase are also available priced at £15.00 for Children, £10.00 for Adults and £7.50 for Senior Citizens. Group discounts are also available.

Detailed Directions by Car:

From the North: Exit the M1 at Junction 19 and take the A14 towards Kettering. Leave the A14 at Junction 10 and follow signs for Wicksteed Park. Alternatively take the A1 to Stamford, the A43 to Kettering then the A14 as above; From the South: Exit the M1 at Junction 15 and take the A43 to the junction with the A14, then as above. Alternatively take the A1 to the Junction with the A14 then continue to Junction 10 as above.

WILLOW WOOD RAILWAY

Address: Woodseaves Garden Plants, Sydnall Lane Nursery, Woodseaves, Market Drayton TF9 2AS
Telephone Nº: (01630) 653161
Year Formed: 2004
Location of Line: Shropshire
Length of Line: 400 yards

Nº of Steam Locos: None
Nº of Other Locos: 1
Nº of Members: –
Approx Nº of Visitors P.A.: Not known
Gauge: 7¼ inches
Web site: www.woodseavesplants.co.uk/railway

GENERAL INFORMATION

Nearest Mainline Station: Shrewsbury (19 miles)
Nearest Bus Station: Market Drayton (3 miles)
Car Parking: Available on site
Coach Parking: A small amount of space available
Souvenir Shop(s): None
Food & Drinks: None

SPECIAL INFORMATION

The railway is constantly evolving with extensions to the track and additions to stock and infrastructure. The railway is currently looking for a narrow gauge steam locomotive.

OPERATING INFORMATION

Opening Times: Sundays from Spring to early Autumn, 10.30am to 4.00pm. Also on some Saturdays and Bank Holidays. Please contact the railway for further details.
Steam Working: None at present
Prices: £1.00 per ride

Detailed Directions by Car:
From All Parts: The railway is located just off the A529 at Woodseaves which is situated approximately 2 miles south of Market Drayton.

WOLVERHAMPTON & DISTRICT M.E.S.

Address: Baggeridge Country Park, Near Sedgley, Staffordshire
Telephone N°: (01902) 753795
Year Formed: 1986
Location: Baggeridge Country Park
Length of Line: Ground level line is a fifth of a mile, the raised track is 420 feet

N° of Steam Locos: 15
N° of Other Locos: 7
N° of Members: 60
Approx N° of Visitors P.A.: Not known
Gauge: 3½ inches, 5 inches & 7¼ inches

GENERAL INFORMATION

Nearest Mainline Station: Wolverhampton (7 miles)
Nearest Bus Station: Sedgley (2 miles)
Car Parking: Available on site
Coach Parking: Available on site
Food & Drinks: Available

SPECIAL INFORMATION

The Wolverhampton & District Model Engineering Society operates the railway which runs through the Baggeridge Country Park. This was formerly the Baggeridge Colliery and part of the original Himley Estate of the Earls of Dudley. Since the closure of the Colliery, the site has been transformed into 150 acres of attractive country park.

OPERATING INFORMATION

Opening Times: Every other Sunday from April to September. Please phone the Secretary for more precise information. Trains run from 11.00am to 5.00pm.
Steam Working: Most operating days.
Prices: No charge but donations are accepted.

Detailed Directions by Car:
Take the A449 Wolverhampton to Kidderminster road then turn onto the A463 towards Sedgley. Baggeridge Country Park is just to the South of the A463 after approximately 2 miles and it is well-signposted from the road.

WYTHALL MINIATURE STEAM RAILWAY

Address: The Transport Museum, Chapel Lane, Wythall, Birmingham, B47 6JX
Telephone Nº: (01564) 826471
Year Formed: 1980s
Location of Line: The Transport Museum, Wythall
Length of Line: 945 feet

Nº of Steam Locos: Members locos
Nº of Other Locos: Members locos
Nº of Members: Approximately 30
Approx Nº of Visitors P.A.: Not known
Gauge: 3½ inches, 5 inches & 7¼ inches
Web site: www.wythallsteamrail.co.uk

GENERAL INFORMATION

Nearest Mainline Station: Wythall (2 miles)
Nearest Bus Station: Birmingham (8 miles)
Car Parking: Available on site
Coach Parking: Available on site
Souvenir Shop: Yes (not specifically railway oriented)
Food & Drinks: Available on event days only

SPECIAL INFORMATION

The railway is operated by members of the Elmdon Model Engineering Society and is sited at the museum site of the Birmingham & Midland Omnibus Trust. See www.bammot.org.uk for details.

OPERATING INFORMATION

Opening Times: The Museum itself is open every weekend from Easter until the end of November. The railway operates on the following dates in 2010: 2nd, 3rd, 30th & 31st May; 20th June (Fathers Day); 29th & 30th August and 10th October.
Steam Working: Every operating day.
Prices: Adult Entrance Fee £4.00
Child Entrance Fee £2.00
Family Ticket Entrance Fee £10.00
Train Rides: 50p per ride (£1.80 for a 4-ride ticket)
Note: An entrance fee is charged for the Museum itself which is required to use the railway.
The railway can cater for Birthday parties by prior arrangement throughout the year.

Detailed Directions by Car:
Wythall is situated on the A435 Alcester to Birmingham road near to Junction 3 of the M42. If travelling from the South, turn left at the roundabout upon reaching Wythall and the Museum is signposted from there. Turn right at this roundabout if travelling from the North.
